Creating an information service

Sylvia P. Webb

D0612888

Second edition

DUQUESNE UNIVERSITY LIBRARY

£9.50

Creating an information service

By the same author:

Personal development in information work (Aslib, 1986)

Creating an information service

Sylvia P. Webb

Second edition

Published by Aslib, The Association for Information Management, 26–27 Boswell Street, London WC1N 3JZ

© Sylvia P. Webb 1983, 1985, 1988

All rights reserved

First published 1983
Reprinted with amendments 1985
Reprinted 1986, 1987
Second edition 1988

British Library Cataloguing in Publication Data

Webb, Sylvia P.
　Creating an information service. — 2nd ed.
　1. Information services. Organisation
　I. Title II. Aslib
　025.5′2

　ISBN 0-85142-237-3

Phototypeset in 10/12 point Plantin by Getset (BTS) Ltd, Eynsham, Oxford
Printed and bound in Great Britain by Henry Ling Ltd at the Dorset Press, Dorchester, Dorset

Z 674.4
ω 4
1988 x

Contents

List of checklists   vi

List of illustrations   vii

Acknowledgements   viii

Introduction   ix

1   Getting to know the organisation   1

2   Existing information resources: internal and external   8

3   Setting up the initial service   15

4   Physical planning   30

5   Making the most of technology   38

6   Procedures and records: what is required?   50

7   Stock: selection, sources and effective use   56

8   Stock: acquisition and processing   64

9   Classification and cataloguing   73

10 Stock: loan and circulation   82

11 Staff: development, qualities and skills   91

12 What next? – future developments   97

Appendices
1   Organisations to approach for information (including special interest groups)   104
2   Organisations offering short courses in library and information work and
    related subjects   113
3   Specialist publishers and book and periodical suppliers   115
4   Library equipment suppliers   119

Index   120

APR 4 1991

Checklists

1	The organisation	2
2	Information needs analysis	6
3	Existing library resources	9
4	Immediate action	20
5	Physical planning	31
6	Typical stock and equipment to be considered when planning a library	36
7	How to find out about information technology	39
8	Online databases – evaluation criteria	42
9	What to include in a manual of procedures	51
10	Book suppliers: typical questions to ask	72
11	Selecting a classification scheme	80

Illustrations

Multi-purpose shelf unit	33
Rotary stand	34
Study carrels	35
Initial circulation note	57
Order form	65
Order card	66
Order slip	67
Page from accessions register	68
Prepared book	71
Cataloguing slip	76
Single record book card	83
Loan slip	84
Multi-part loan slip	85
Visible index card and slip	86
External loan slip	87
Journal circulation slip	88
Approval slip	89
Stock review form	89
How to trace UK company information	99

Acknowledgements

I would like to thank those organisations and individuals who have allowed their products and services to be mentioned. Thanks are also due to Alan Macgregor and his colleagues at the British Library Information Sciences Service (successor to the Library Association Library), and to the staff of the Information Resources Centre at Aslib, for their co-operation and assistance.

Introduction

What is offered here is an approach, a positive and practical way of setting about the task of establishing a library or information service, often with little assistance in terms of support staff. It therefore has particular relevance to those working as one person libraries, i.e. those running a service single handed, and those who may have little experience in the operation of special libraries. It looks especially at business and professional libraries in the United Kingdom, but the general principles described could as easily apply to any small specialist collection of information.

This book does not represent an attempt to re-invent the wheel. Where an in-depth knowledge of a subject or technique is required, then one of the many detailed texts already in existence should be consulted.

The emphasis is on simplicity and efficiency in all the procedures and techniques discussed, and real-life examples of the ways in which certain problems have been handled in specific libraries are included. A number of checklists have been devised as ways of clearing the ground. They answer some questions and suggest others that need to be asked, in order that an information service most appropriate to the needs of the organisation is developed; one which is not seen in isolation but as an integral part of that organisation's business activities.

The use of the computer does not necessarily preclude the use of manual procedures. Both have their place; you must choose which is the most appropriate for each purpose, given the specific environment in which you are establishing your service.

Although the word 'librarian' is used throughout it should be interpreted as meaning anyone organising an information service.

The book suggests further reading where more detail may be required, as well as indicating where to go and who to contact for further assistance.

1 • *Getting to know the organisation*

When joining a new organisation, or taking on a new role within an organisation which is already known, it is essential to go in with an open mind and a high degree of imagination. These two qualities backed by constant enthusiasm and unflagging energy will certainly be needed, especially during the first six months of taking on the job of setting up a library or information service; particularly when it is in the field of business or professional information where the emphasis is always on 'instant information'. (If that has not already put you off, please read on!)

The first thing to do, often the most difficult, is to draw up some sort of guideline as to what the organisation has in mind; what is the main purpose of having a library, and what is hoped will come out of it? Often the library has been, or is being, established because 'it seemed like a good idea' or, equally vague, 'it is time we had a library'. It could, however, be the result of more positive thinking, and the realisation that the organisation needs information regularly, and is aware that having a central point of reference for information enquiries is likely to be more efficient and effective than the 'shot in the dark' approach. This approach still exists, with each person in the organisation desperately trying to think who to ring when there is a sudden need for information vital to the business. Everyone in the organisation does *not* know the sources of information which exist, nor which would be the most appropriate to approach.

The first step towards drawing up some guidelines on the type of library needed is to get to know something about the organisation itself: how big it is; what its objectives are; the nature of its business; the main subject areas that relate to its business activities. Some of these questions may have been answered in part during the appointment interview, or be outlined in a publicity brochure, but it is always worth putting together a simple organisational profile as soon as possible. This will act as a starting point towards understanding the organisation and identifying its information requirements.

The best way of starting off is to go around the organisation as soon as possible and make personal contact with its members. This should be seen as a two-part procedure. The first of the two visits is one in which short introductory contact is made, but expectation is set for the second visit, which will be a follow-up with a more specific purpose, i.e. to see what particular information needs each individual or department has. It is important to carry out this follow-up visit fairly quickly, while its purpose (and your face!) is still remembered.

It will be very helpful if the circulation of a note about you has preceded your arrival, but if not, useful early communication with members of the organisation can be made by sending around a memorandum after the first visit, and before the second. The purpose of this is to reinforce the first contact and to introduce yourself to those people with whom contact was not made on the first visit; also to make some general statements about the service it is hoped to provide. It is, however, important at this stage not to be committed to specific procedures until there has been time to assess what is needed. This communication can also be used as the means of explaining the purpose of, and setting up, the second visit.

As this is the first written communication from the new librarian its style is important. It should, as is sometimes said of computer software, be 'user-friendly'! The aim of a business library should be to be useful and used. However comprehensive the stock, and professionally qualified the staff, a positive and helpful response to enquiries certainly seems to bring about increased use of the service. This in turn assists the librarian in ascertaining the direction in which to develop it further, and in doing so to create an information service most appropriate to the organisation's activities.

Before carrying out the series of second visits, which will act as the basis for an analysis of information needs and will vary in the degree of formality according to each organisation and the time available, it is a good idea to put together the organisational profile previously mentioned. The following checklist may be helpful:

Checklist 1: The organisation (Part 1)

(1) Type of business activity and clientele
(2) Possible related subject areas
(3) Number of sites, e.g. other offices and associates
(4) Location of sites
(5) Total number of staff by location (these are all potential library users)
(6) Number of staff by function, e.g. number of partners, managers, consultants, specialists, researchers, administrative and secretarial staff
(7) Number and type of separate departments (to include size and special interests)

Information on these seven items should be easily obtainable from (a) organisational literature and (b) other staff in the department. An extension of this checklist can be drawn up for use on the second visit, and will be completed by (a) observation and (b) questions to appropriate departments. The items covered in the second part of the checklist relate to the existence and use of communal resources as follows:

Checklist 1: The organisation (Part 2)

  (8) Photocopying machines:
      (a) location
      (b) type, e.g.
        — reducing/enlarging facility
        — paper size available
        — quality
  (9) Typing services
      — centralised or departmental
(10) Printing services
      — in-house and/or external
      — how long does printing usually take
(11) Stationery
      — what is available, where and when
(12) Computer and word processor facilities
      — how widely available are they
(13) Projectors, screens and audiovisual material
      — location
      — type
      — who prepares slides, etc.
(14) Telex and facsimile document/printer services
      — location
(15) Microfilm/microfiche readers
      — location
      — main use
      — type, e.g. is it a reader/printer
In each case try to get a personal name, so that you know who to approach when you need any of these services

---

This two-part checklist, combined with the experience of your first few days in the organisation, should take you on to the next stage. This is to make some analysis of the information needs of the organisation. If you have in fact taken on a new role to become librarian, but were already working with the organisation, then you have the advantage of already being familiar with its objectives and business activities. It is, however, just as useful to carry out the information needs analysis. As well as establishing what is required of a new information service, or what changes may be necessary in an existing library, the act of carrying out the analysis helps to establish you in your new role.

The information needs analysis

This is particularly necessary where a library has not previously existed within the organisation, or where radical change to an existing service is planned. The following example is of a firm operating as a partnership, and the job titles are therefore those used in such an organisation. The example is equally appropriate to other organisations and all that will need changing will be the job titles or names of departments.

Taking a firm with about 30 partners and a larger number of managers, it will be found that each partner has responsibility for certain activities, e.g. training, consultancy, as well as for work with particular clients. These activities and client work will mean, therefore, that each partner will have certain subject interests, which may or may not overlap with those of other partners. In addition to such specialist interests, some subjects will be of general concern, such as those of developments in the particular profession or business on which the organisation is based, e.g. law, accountancy, property.

The term 'manager' in this context means someone who is professionally qualified and works in a particular team headed by a partner. In a company this could equally be someone with specialist skills working in a department headed by a general manager or director. He or she will therefore share certain subject interests with that partner, as well as having individual professional interests. The manager will also probably have responsibility for a number of trainee and other junior staff.

This simplified picture of the main potential users of the library deliberately concentrates on the professional staff. There are a number of administrative and secretarial staff who are also likely to be regular library users, but their information requirements will either be in the same business subject areas, or will be of a general nature to be answered from the basic reference stock.

The purpose of the information needs analysis is to establish the main areas in which information will be sought, and to set up an appropriate collection of resources to satisfy those needs. Such resources will not all be on site; most business libraries rely almost as much on external sources of information as on internal resources.

It is usual to carry out an information needs analysis either by personal interview or by questionnaire. The former is the preferred method as (a) it gives the librarian the opportunity to establish a rapport with the people for whom he or she is setting up the information service and (b) it helps the members of the organisation to think constructively about their real information requirements.

The questionnaire can be used where personal meetings are difficult to arrange, e.g. for associate offices located in another part of the country, or for those people who are often out of the office. Checklist 2 can easily be adapted as a questionnaire.

The essence of this exercise is for each interview to be brief – time is money in business – but comprehensive enough to serve its purpose. Ten to fifteen minutes is adequate and makes it much more likely that a partner will be able to see you. It can be useful to see together a partner and a manager from the same team.

Set up the interview by telephoning the partner's secretary and saying that you are trying to see all the partners over the next week or so to discuss their particular requirements in relation to the new library. Emphasise that you will not take more than ten to fifteen minutes of their time. If you have already sent a memorandum around, then the partner and the secretary will be familiar with the idea that such interviews are being set up.

Try to find out about each partner's responsibilities well in advance of the interview. There will then be some understanding of the partner's role in the organisation. Such details may be available in, for example, a brochure handed out to new recruits; or may be discovered by talking to someone who has been with the organisation long enough to be familiar with such information.

Make a brief note of the points to be covered in the interview. This is essential if the interview is to be kept short and the overall series to be comparable. The main things to establish at such an interview could be set out as shown, with the first part completed as far as possible before the interview. Draw up the checklist with appropriate spaces for responses and make duplicate copies. A tick or a one word answer on the checklist will help the interview to flow and to be kept within the stated time limit.

Also think up an opening statement for the interview. For example: 'Before committing the firm to any expenditure, I want to carry out some sort of analysis of what information is required and what resources already exist in-house. In that way I am hoping to avoid duplication, as far as possible, in terms of stock and, of course, staff time.'

A common question at such interviews is: 'When is the service going to start?' The best answer is always a positive one, which suggests that you are there and will be happy to try and answer any questions which they have *as from now*. It is most important to encourage enquiries and offer a service at the earliest possible stage. This can be achieved even without having any stock. Local external sources can be used; a telephone call can provide the answer to a number of simple enquiries. Other librarians are usually very sympathetic to the situation and will often volunteer anything from sending a photocopy in response to a particular enquiry, to offering earlier editions of books and back runs of journals which they may be going to discard.

Wind up the interview by saying that as soon as you have completed the interviews, and analysed the responses, you will be sending around a memorandum, outlining the service that you hope to provide, and when it will be fully operational. A target date generates confidence that a library service will

Checklist 2: Information needs analysis

Name of Partner: Name of Secretary:

Location of Office:

Main Responsibilities:

(1) Type of information required regularly by subject areas and format (amend to suit your organisation's interests):

(a) company information
(b) industry or sector information
(c) economic information
(d) financial information
(e) management information
(f) developments in, e.g. law
                              accountancy
                              property

} likely to be in the form of statistics, press comment, annual reports, updating services

(g) other specific areas

(2) Is the emphasis likely to be more on current or historical information:
(3) Which newspapers and journals are read regularly:
(4) Any other publications received regularly, e.g. annual reports, cuttings service, etc.:
(5) Any reference books consulted regularly:
    Are these used as office workbooks, i.e. required to be kept as an office copy; if so, should they be duplicated in the library?
(6) Any subject files maintained in office/department:
(7) Databases consulted regularly:
(8) Membership of any professional organisation which (a) could be used to get publications at reduced prices or (b) would mean that its library could be used as a further source of information:
(9) Could any of the material which has been discussed usefully be transferred to the library:
(10) Other comments:
    (Other information may be volunteered, i.e. committee membership; involvement in any of the firm's own publications; review copies received which may be donated to the library; directories which may carry any entry for the firm and therefore be available at a reduced price; the fact that one of the clerks has been providing a cuttings service, etc.)

be available soon, and helps members of the firm to tolerate, and give support during, the interim period.

This period should be as short as possible, although administrative timetables in existence may affect this, e.g. dates on which certain committees meet. It may be that certain committees have to approve each stage of the project. On the other hand, such decisions may be the responsibility of an individual; an initial arbitrary budget may have already been agreed.

It is also important that in this intial stage the job of setting up the library does not become too complex. It would take too long and could prevent the offering of even a limited enquiry service, which, as has been said, is very valuable in setting the long-term image of helpfulness and usefulness of the library. People need to get into the habit of using the new library, which they will only do if they get some positive responses to their enquiries.

When the interviews have been carried out, a simple analysis of the responses will reveal certain subjects in which there is a general interest; some which are of interest to a few people or only one department; and others which may be relevant to only one person's work. From this, an overall list of subjects to be covered by the library service can be drawn up.

The existence of any in-house publications, some of which may be produced or revised regularly, will also indicate subject interests. Committees may or may not have particular information requirements, e.g. client relations committees, training committees.

The reading patterns and existence of subject files will be useful in indicating some of the newspaper and journal requirements of the new library, as well as helping to assess the amount of scanning that needs to be done by the librarian, avoiding unnecessary duplication. Subject files already in use may or may not need to be duplicated in the library, or could be integrated into a central collection of information files. They will also provide strong indicators for the use of online or the setting up of internal databases (see Chapter 5).

It may already have been suggested by those interviewed that certain office or departmental collections of reference books and other material should remain in the department as working collections, or that they could be transferred to the library. This knowledge will help in the drawing up of a basic list of essential material, which will form the nucleus of the new library, and in deciding how much to use external sources of information. The information on partners' and managers' membership of other organisations will relate to the last point. The degree of reliance on external resources will be discussed in the next chapter.

2 • Existing information resources: internal and external

Having looked at the organisation, found out about in-house resources generally, and done some analysis of the information requirements, the next step is to try to co-ordinate the information resources that already exist, whether these are in the form of an established library, or individual collections and resources scattered throughout the organisation. The results of such co-ordination will form the basis of the proposed new service.

The previous chapter considered the organisation as a whole; in this chapter I will be focusing more specifically on the library: what there is at present in terms of stock, staff, equipment and procedures, what can be centrally co-ordinated, and what use can be made of external resources.

The existing library

In the case of an already established library which is going to be developed in new directions, there are a number of questions to be asked, some of which may already have been answered by the use of the earlier checklists. Such questions could again usefully be organised in checklist form, although it will be somewhat lengthier than the previous checklists.

Other information resources

Having looked at the existing library, the next step is to list other information collections located elsewhere in the organisation. This should be something which has already been learned from the information needs analysis and will involve a straight listing by subject to see how each collection relates to the existing library coverage, and whether there is any overlap or duplication of material.

Checklist 3: Existing library resources

(1) Location and overall organisation

Where is the library physically located; is this a permanent or temporary location; is it part of another department?

Does the library have certain hours of opening; can it operate only when library staff are there or does it work on a self-service basis; is the stock mainly for reference or for loan; are there study facilities; do enquirers usually visit the library personally, or are most enquiries by telephone; what sort of overall service has been given, e.g. have any library bulletins or newsletters been published on a regular basis, are newspapers and journals scanned for any selective provision of information, or for other purposes; has the full service been extended to associate offices and other 'off-site' staff; what reliance has there been on external resources; are any of these used regularly; does the library co-operate by providing any services to other libraries?

(2) Stock

Subject coverage

How does this relate to the requirements expressed in the information needs analysis; how historical or current is the coverage; is there any foreign language material?

Format

What is the present emphasis, e.g. books, journals, subject files, microfilm/fiche, online services, maps, audiovisual material, special collections (e.g. company/technical reports)?

In-house publications

Is there a collection or stock of these?

Physical organisation

What shelving, filing cabinets, hanging files, storage boxes and other related storage facilities are there? How is material identified, e.g. by stamping and labelling?

Stock check

Has there been one; is this carried out regularly?

Classification

Which scheme is in use; is it used for all material?

Continued overleaf

Continued from previous page

Catalogue
(a) What physical form is this in, e.g. card, book, printed loose-leaf lists, microfiche, computerised?
(b) How is it arranged, e.g. by author, title, subject or in one alphabetical sequence, i.e. a dictionary catalogue?
(c) Does it include journal holdings and other serial publications?
(d) Is there any manual of the classification and cataloguing procedures?
(e) Are catalogue entries prepared in-house or bought in?

Loan system (including circulation)
If there is loan stock, how are loans recorded; is there any date limit; is there a loan recall system; are all types of material available for loan; is there any circulation of material such as journals or new books; how is circulation controlled; are there arrangements for interlibrary loan, e.g. are there any British Library loan forms, etc.

Abstracts and indexes
Are there any abstracting or indexing services, either those produced commercially such as *Anbar Management Abstracts* (printed), *Research Index* (online); or have any been produced internally?

Selection and purchase of stock
Who selects new material, e.g. the librarian, other staff, a committee; what sources are used as a basis for selection, e.g. suggestions from users, reviews and lists in newspapers and journals, regular visits to bookshops, personalised book supplier service; are there standing orders for certain essential material; does one book supplier supply everything or are there a number of suppliers; are items usually ordered on approval?

(3) Administration and administrative procedures
The budget
Was or is there a separate library budget; who has overall responsibility for it?

Invoices and orders
Who has authority to sign these; what records have been kept; how are such records organised and for what period of time do they need to be maintained?

Correspondence and memoranda
What copies are kept, where, and for how long?

Manual of administrative procedures
Is there one; what does it cover? (It may answer a number of questions on the checklist.)

Enquiry forms
Are they, or have they been, used; what sort of information do they give?

(4) **Furniture and equipment**
Work surfaces
What desks, tables and work-tops are there for library staff and library users?

Seating
What sort of seating exists, e.g. desks, chairs, armchairs?

Equipment
What equipment is there in the library, e.g. telephone, typewriter, photocopier, fax machine, microfiche or microfilm reader/printer, projector, word processor, computer; and what is their main purpose for being there?.

(5) **Lighting, heating, ventilation and other environmental factors**
Lighting
How much natural light is there and how much supplementary artificial light; are there individual desk lights; are there ceiling and/or wall lights; are the lights able to be controlled on a variable basis or are they operated by only one or a few switches?

Heating and ventilation
What form of heating exists; is it individually controllable; is there air-conditioning; are there windows which can be opened; is there any other form of ventilation, e.g. electric fans, ventilation panels, etc.; is any of the equipment/stock required to be kept at special temperatures?

General environment
What is the floor surface; does this affect noise level; can external noise be heard in the library and to what level of disturbance; are there doors

Continued overleaf

Continued from previous page

leading directly to other departments, possibly causing the library to be a through-way; are there windows with an external view; what is the overall impression on entering the library, e.g. attractive, comfortable, well set out, easy-to-use, conducive to study, etc.?

(6) Staff

How many; are they full- or part-time; what range of skills do they have; what support is there from other departments or sections, e.g. in the form of secretarial and clerical services of a permanent, temporary or occasional nature; what opportunities are there for staff training and development; what tasks are performed, by whom; any use of subject specialists inside and outside the department; of what professional groups are the library staff members; what degree of involvement is there with staff of other libraries?

The original analysis should also have indicated whether such collections need to be kept by individuals or departments as working tools, or whether they could usefully be transferred to the library. The same questions about stock will need to be asked as suggested under Section 2 of Checklist 3: Existing library resources. Even if the collections are to be kept by the departments, it is still useful for the department or the individual to be kept informed of any new editions or other new material in that subject area. The library should have a central listing of the items in these collections so that the whole organisation can be aware of their availability. This can be easily achieved where there is a computer network, with screens throughout the building.

In the case of there being no previous library in existence such collections are most important as they represent the only stock available within the organisation. A central listing of this material, however simple, will be invaluable when deciding on the initial basic collection required in setting up the new information service, and will offer some means, however limited, of answering enquiries in the early stages.

In this initial period it is essential to make early contact with other libraries, as they will be another important resource. The Existing library resources Checklist will show under Section 1 whether any network of contacts with other libraries has already been established.

The information needs analysis will have indicated membership of certain organisations, and the existence of a library or information service within such organisations may also have been mentioned. If not, then the *Directory of British associations* should be consulted, possibly in the nearest public library. This directory (which is recommended as part of the core collection of reference books given in Chapter 3) lists organisations alphabetically by name, and indexes them by subject interest. If a library or information service exists, this will be shown among other details under the main entry.

If you are setting up a library for a firm providing a professional service then it is likely that a high proportion of the people within the firm will be members of a particular professional association, e.g. the Institute of Chartered Accountants, the Royal Institution of Chartered Surveyors. This gives access to a whole range of services of such organisations, including the library, therefore such associations should be the first with whom contact is made, along with your nearest public library, which can be traced through the local telephone directory.

Apart from the associations, librarians of other firms in the same business field can be very helpful, having experienced the same, or similar, problems as those which you may encounter.

Make a list of about a dozen such firms (the professional association would be a good source for names as they are likely to know whether a firm has a library or not, and possibly be able to give a personal name to contact); then telephone the librarian of each firm and ask if it would be possible to visit the library and ask some questions, explaining your reason for doing so.

Always have in mind that time is valuable, both to you and the other librarian involved, and limit the visit accordingly. Perhaps set up two or three visits for one morning where the libraries are geographically close and spend an hour at each. Most importantly, decide what you need to know before you go.

The headings of the Existing library resources Checklist can be used as a basis for your questions, although it is necessary to modify the detail listed under those headings. The emphasis of these questions will be on what sort of information is most regularly required; what stock is, or has been, found to be most useful; and the procedures in use. A number of questions on layout and physical organisation will be answered by observation.

It is a good idea just to ask the librarian a broad question on the range of services provided and then to listen and make notes on the various items. After listening you can then ask specific questions on any areas not covered.

It is useful to make a written summary of these visits as soon as possible after each visit has taken place. Apart from not having to rely on memory, such summaries are useful in a number of ways. They will help you to get a feel for the subject areas in context, and to put into perspective your own ideas of what is required for the new library. Insights will have been gained on matters such as budgets, staffing, etc. If a report or proposal concerning the development of the new library is required, the summaries serve as excellent examples of directions and procedures which have already proved to be useful in firms with similar objectives. Above all you will have met a number of librarians with professional interests similar to your own. Such networks often develop into informal 'self-help' groups, through which the members are able to meet and discuss common problems as well as float new ideas for comment. Examples of these in the United Kingdom are the Bank Librarians Group, the Accounting Librarians Group, the City Information Group and the One Man Bands Group, which has gone on to become a formal Aslib group. There are others which are listed in Appendix 1.

Formal groups with various subject interests, such as the Aslib groups and those of the Library Association and the Institute of Information Scientists, also provide the opportunity to meet colleagues with similar information interests. In the field of business information the two most useful are the Aslib Economic & Business Information Group (AEBIG) and the Library Association Industrial Group (LAIG). They hold regular meetings as well as organising courses and seminars on topics of interest. They also publish their own newsletters on current developments.

These groups will be mentioned further in Chapter 12 and Appendix 1 but they do form a valuable part of the whole area of external resources, upon which many libraries depend, in order to be able to offer a comprehensive service. The range and availability of external resources will play an important part in determining what sort of service you are going to set up for your organisation.

Further reading

JACKSON, P. *British sources of information: a subject guide and bibliography*. London: Routledge & Kegan Paul, 1987.
Who's who in the UK information world 1988/89. London: TFPL Publishing, 1988.

3 • *Setting up the initial service*

Information has now been collected on what the organisation requires, what resources are already there, and what can be obtained from external sources. It is time to put all this information together, see what else is required and start setting up the new service.

It is most important at this stage not to be over-ambitious. Start with a small, initial collection, from which enquiries can be answered, and get the service off the ground. Gaining the confidence of users is most important at this stage. They do not want to have to wait too long for the new service: their expectations have been set, they have already given time and thought to their information needs. So start giving them a service by answering their enquiries.

At this stage the considerations are short-term. Set up the initial service and test it, before spending too much money or time; see what the demands are and what the most helpful responses might be; then think of the service on a longer-term basis. All procedures such as indexing or classification should be kept simple and flexible to allow for the development of the service.

This means that, as far as classification and cataloguing are concerned, if there is already a system in use which is acceptable, then continue to use it, at least for the time being. If you have not inherited a classification scheme, or where there is no previous stock, then consider whether a formal classification is necessary, e.g. a simple series of keywords has been found to be more appropriate in some libraries. Where a classification scheme is needed, look at those already in use in other libraries; select one that has been tried out and tested. Few, if any, classification schemes could be said to be perfect for all requirements, so take one that is straightforward and which has proved satisfactory in a similar library. Particularly in the case of one person libraries the scheme needs to be practical and easy-to-run, from the point of view of ease-of-classification in terms of the librarian's time and ease-of-use for the enquirer, especially if the library is being set up to run on a 'self-service' basis.

If there is an existing library collection, do not attempt too much revision at first. Test its usefulness over a period of time, at least six months, before starting to weed out less relevant items, apart from those which are obviously out-of-date and therefore misleading, or those in subject areas which are no longer relevant to the firm's interests.

There are two important things to keep in mind at this stage. The first is to maintain contact with users. Let them know what sort of service they can expect. As soon as possible, circulate a progress report stating what has been carried out so far – i.e. information needs analysis, visits to other libraries, the setting up of a network of contacts – and outlining the initial scheme envisaged.

This is the stage, i.e. within the first month, at which some librarians have found it appropriate to make a presentation to members of the organisation, either as a follow-up to, or instead of, the circulation of the progress report. Such presentations need to be well-prepared, as they act as publicity for the new service. They must be seen to have a purpose, i.e. to give further information about the service; they should have a stated duration and some sort of summary which can be handed out as an *aide-mémoire* to those attending.

The purpose of a presentation of this kind is to make a statement about the potential role of the library and information service within the organisation. One librarian found that a useful way to do this was to make a brief list of the functions to which the library could usefully contribute; also a list of criteria by which the service should be judged, i.e. quality, efficiency and accessibility. These criteria are particularly important as they determine the way in which the whole service will be developed.

Setting up a presentation involves determining a date and time when most potential users of the service are able to come. This can be done by circulating a memo, offering several dates, then following this with a note stating the finally agreed time and place. The note will also act as a reminder to attendees.

Presentations can be carried out in the library, which can act as its own visual aid (for better or worse!), but at this early stage a separate room with an overhead projector and comfortable seating is preferable. An online demonstration can also add a lot to the presentation. If the end of the formal presentation can be co-ordinated with coffee or tea, this adds an opportunity for further informal discussion, and liaison with users.

The presentation and the progress report both offer the opportunity for further personal contact. You can say that you would now like to come and collect the various items which have been offered for the central stock. Personal visits of this sort are important as they give you the opportunity to meet the users again, and to re-establish yourself as being there in an active role. Some of your initial enquiries will occur during these visits, giving some practical indication of the type of stock and service required. They also give the librarian the opportunity to demonstrate at an early stage how useful the new service can be.

The second important matter requiring action is deciding on, and acquiring as quickly as possible, the initial stock which, with that already available, will form the nucleus of the new service. Publications already noted as being in regular use in other similar libraries will form part of this core collection. Other items may be those which you have personally found to be essential basic reference books in your previous work. Send for publishers' catalogues and scan them. The relevant professional associations may have compiled subject lists of books and journals which will act as useful sources on which selection can be based, although it is important to note the dates of such lists, so that material under consideration is known to be as up-to-date as possible.

A well-organised and easy-to-use guide to general directory-type reference books is *The top 3000 directories and annuals*, produced by Alan Armstrong Ltd. This is a very good starting point for selection as, although the entries are brief, they give essential details such as when the current edition was published and when the next edition is due, as well as subject coverage, publisher and price. Apart from the main sequence, which is alphabetical by title, there is also a subject index, and a list of publishers showing which reference books each produces. Although there are other, more comprehensive, guides to reference material, which give much more detailed entries on a greater number of publications (e.g. *Walford's guide to reference material*), as a quick source of up-to-date information the Armstrong directory is well worth consulting.

From these various sources draw up a core list of approximately 100 essential reference books and perhaps 25–30 journal titles. A large number of these will be of a general nature, with additional specialist titles according to the organisation's business interests. Although this may sound like a rather small collection in terms of number of titles, it should consist of items of maximum usefulness. For example, the *Directory of British associations*, mentioned in Chapter 2, acts as a guide to an extremely wide range of other sources of information, as does the *Aslib directory of information sources in the UK* and the *Libraries, museums & art galleries yearbook*, all of which are mentioned in the suggested core-list at the end of this chapter.

Apart from usefulness and quality-rather-than-quantity considerations, there is also the matter of the budget. There will be other areas in which expenditure is required in this initial period, e.g. shelving, equipment, stationery, possibly temporary staff, so the purchase of stock *per se* needs to be balanced against these, and stock which can be easily consulted elsewhere. Drawing up the initial budget is not just a matter of listing items or services for which payment will have to be made. It also involves justifying that expenditure which, in the case of a new or expanded department is additional to the organisation's previous overall budget. Keep the layout simple and, where additional explanation is desirable, give this in the form of a short, clear note. Accompanying notes are best presented on a separate page so that they can be read in conjunction with the figures.

Costs are likely to fall under three main headings:

— Staff – this will consist largely of salary costs, not forgetting to make provision for any temporary assistance which may be required in the setting-up process, e.g. for data input. Some indication of training costs should also be included, even if it is envisaged that this may take place at a later stage. It will underline the importance of this area.

— Stock — this heading can be usefully broken down by the type of resource, which will be helpful in future reviews of expenditure for planning purposes. It should also include related costs such as printing, online manuals and specialist stationery, if this is not met centrally as part of the overall organisational budget.

— Equipment — Checklist 3 will have indicated what is already available in-house, but any items which are to be ordered specifically for the new unit should be shown here. They should be regarded as one-off items of capital expenditure, unlikely to appear as a regular heading, unless over a period of time they need replacing or upgrading. It could be useful to show the costs of any related installation and maintenance contracts unless again these costs are carried centrally. When considering the cost of a microcomputer do not overlook related requirements, e.g. modem, screen, printer.

Future budgets may well need to include an additional heading for any recoverable costs, e.g. by charging for staff time or for specific services. Your budget must be prepared with a specific audience in mind — those you want to influence into agreeing its content. 'If you want your ideas approved' is an article worth reading in this context. You may also find the video 'Everything is negotiable' helpful. A comprehensive treatment of costing and budgeting for libraries is provided by Stephen Roberts in *Cost management for library and information services*. A useful journal offering practical articles of all aspects of managing a library, relevant to all special libraries, not just those in the business environment, is *Business Library Management*.

Having drawn up the core-list, check against it any material already donated or promised by other people in the organisation, or by other libraries. Make a note of any discounts which may be available due to advertisements or entries placed in publications by the organisation, or due to professional memberships. It is equally important to try and avoid buying publications which have already been used and found to be unreliable sources or unsuitable in some other way. Attention may already have been drawn to these in the course of the various visits made to other libraries.

It could be worth circulating this core-list around the firm with such notes as have been made, and asking for any further details of donations, discounts, etc. which are not already noted, but which will assist in making best use of the initial expenditure on the new service. If you do circulate the list, remember to add a note to the effect that it would be helpful if it could be returned with any extra details by a particular date, so that the stock can be ordered and the library become operational as soon as possible. The tone of all such communications should be positive and business-like, whilst reflecting personal enthusiasm for an early start to the new service.

By this time, contact will already have been made with the librarians of professional associations of which the organisation, or individuals, are members. Now is the time to take up membership of associations and groups which can help you in your role as librarian or information officer. If you are already a member of the Library Association (LA), it could be useful to choose the Industrial Group, the Publicity and Public Relations Group, or the Information Technology Group as the specialist groups to which you can elect to belong.

It could be helpful to seek the advice of an information consultant, as did one particular librarian, in her first professional appointment. This she found extremely useful when setting up a library for a firm of chartered accountants. The consultation consisted of a visit by the consultant to the firm for discussions. As well as a review of the existing stock and comment on the progress report which the firm's librarian had drawn up, advice on various procedures and suggestions for future developments were also given. The firm's librarian found this to be extremely valuable in that it confirmed and clarified her own ideas for the development of the service, and gave her a more confident approach to the task, as well as setting up a point of future reference. A guide to consultants specialising in various fields can be found in *A directory of information brokers and consultants*, mentioned in the core list at the end of the chapter.

During this initial period it could also be valuable to attend one or more of the short courses, seminars or meetings organised by Aslib, the LA, their groups, and other organisations. These are mentioned in more detail in the chapter on staff and staff development, and in Appendix 2. These courses and meetings are time well spent, not only for the formal content, but as opportunities to meet other people working in the same field, experiencing similar problems. It is well worth building up a card index or computer file of these contacts, along with those already made, for future reference. They can prove to be very helpful.

Help, and encouragement, is certainly what will be needed at this time. Without doubt there will be occasions when there are a number of different administrative procedures to be set up, all equally urgent; decisions to be made on stock selection, as well as the shelving and equipment to house the stock; reports to be written; and, at the same time, a helpful information service to be given. It could be said that the order in which the various tasks are carried out is a matter of personal choice — they all have to be done. This is perhaps where a timetable of essential tasks should be drawn up. The progress report will already have been prepared, and can act as a useful indicator, in conjunction with the Existing library resources Checklist and the summary reports of visits to other libraries, of the immediate tasks still to be carried out to make the service operational.

The following typical list of immediate tasks is likely to emerge. Details on what is involved in the various procedures listed are discussed in the appropriate chapters.

Checklist 4: Immediate action

(1) Set up a file in which a note of all procedures is made as the basis for a staff manual

(2) Draw up a list of all possible book suppliers

(3) Set up ordering procedure

(4) Set up correspondence files

(5) Consider budgetary control system, possibly using a spreadsheet package (see Chapter 5)

(6) Order initial stock using core list

(7) Send for sample copies of journals and details of various information services

(8) Decide on arrangement of stock, i.e. formally classified, arranged by keyword, authors, etc. and labelling and identifying methods

(9) Decide on cataloguing procedures

(10) Devise loan and circulation system

(11) Set up methods of recording the arrival of books, journals, looseleaf services, e.g. the use of a visible index, order cards, computer file

(12) Design enquiry form

(13) Look at catalogues of library shelving, equipment, furniture and stationery; assess requirements, and order, having checked that nothing is already available within the organisation

NB: A checklist for the evaluation of online databases and software is given in Chapter 5.

Having drawn up such a list of tasks it is important to assign some realistic dates to their completion. Keep in mind that you want to provide a full information service at the earliest possible date, but that it must be operating efficiently and effectively from that very first day. Deadlines are particularly important where you are dependent on delivery from outside suppliers. Therefore it is worth telephoning suppliers before placing a firm order, and asking their shortest possible delivery time. If they cannot meet your deadline, try another supplier, who may be more keen to get your business.

As new stock starts to arrive it will need to be recorded, identified and arranged according to the systems devised. This will also involve the co-ordination of any existing stock into the same system. In the case of journals, particularly, it may be necessary to refer back to the requirements expressed in the information needs analysis regarding the distribution and circulation of certain titles.

The information needs analysis will also have mentioned other long-term possibilities, such as information bulletins, newsletters, and involvement in various projects, but your concern at this point is getting the service off the ground. The related methods and procedures for doing this will be described in the chapters which follow, after which (having recovered sufficiently) consideration can be given to the wider potential and future of the service.

Further reading

Business Library Management. Cleveland: Headland Press, 8 issues per annum.
DARE, G.A. and BAKEWELL, K.G.B. *The manager's guide to getting answers* (2nd edition). London: Library Association, 1983.
DENTON, D. KEITH If you want your ideas approved. *Management Solutions*, September 1986, 5–11.
'Everything is negotiable'. Video and accompanying materials available for hire or purchase from Guild Sound and Vision (address in Appendix 1).
ROBERTS, S.A. *Cost management for library and information services*. London: Butterworth, 1985.
STOAKLEY, R. *Presenting the library service* London: Clive Bingley, 1982.

CORE LIST OF ESSENTIAL REFERENCE BOOKS AND PERIODICALS

The titles listed below are mainly of a general nature. Specialist titles should be added according to business interest. Newspapers, in particular the *Financial Times*, and the business, economic and technology pages of other daily and Sunday newspapers should also be added. Date of publication is not given for regularly produced titles, instead frequency is shown. 'Looseleaf' indicates titles with an updating service.

Online databases can be selected from the specialist directories listed at the end of Chapter 5.

Reference books

AA Hotels and Restaurants in Britain. Annual. Automobile Association.

ABC Worldwide Hotel Guide. Twice a year. ABC International.

A-Z Master Atlas of Greater London. Geographer's A-Z Map Company, 1987.

Access to parliamentary resources and information in London libraries (3rd edition). House of Commons Library Public Information Office, 1988.

Advertisers Annual. Annual. Thomas Skinner Directories.

Annual Abstract of Statistics. Annual. HMSO.

Aslib directory of information sources in the UK, vol 1 — science, technology and commerce (1982), vol 2 — social sciences, medicine and humanities (1984). Aslib. (Next edition due 1989.)

Aslib Economic and Business Information Group Membership Directory. Annual. Aslib.

Benn's Media Directory. Annual. Benn Business Information Service Ltd.

Blay's guide to regional finance for industry and commerce. Looseleaf. Blay's Guides.

Books in Print. Annual. (Covers virtually all titles published in the United States of America.)

Britain: an Official Handbook. Annual. HMSO.

Britain's Privately Owned Companies: The Top 4000. Annual. Jordan and Sons.

Britain's Top 1000 Foreign Owned Companies. Annual. Jordan and Sons.

British Books in Print, see Whitaker's Books in Print.

British Company Secretary's Practice Manual. Looseleaf. CCH.

British National Bibliography. Weekly, monthly, quarterly and annually. Available in printed form and online. British Library Bibliographic Services Division. (Lists British publications by author and title.)

British Standards Yearbook and Catalogue of Publications. Annual. British Standards Institute.

British Qualifications. Annual. Kogan Page.

British tax cases. Looseleaf. CCH.

British tax guide. Looseleaf. CCH.

British tax legislation. 2 vols. Looseleaf. CCH.

Building Societies Yearbook. Annual. Franey and Co.

Campaign Portfolio. Annual. Marketing Publications. (Lists advertising agencies and their clients.)

Cassell's German/English dictionary. Cassell, 1982.

Cassell's Spanish/English dictionary. Cassell, 1978.

Catalogue of British Official Publications not Published by HMSO. Bi-monthly. Chadwyck-Healey. (Also available online.)

Chartered Institute of Public Finance and Accountancy Local Government Comparative Statistics. Annual. CIPFA.

CICI Directory of information products and services. Longman, 1988.

City Directory. Annual. Woodhead-Faulkner. (A guide to financial and professional services allied to the City of London.)

Civil Service Yearbook. Annual. HMSO.

Commonwealth Universities Yearbook. Annual. Association of Commonwealth Universities.

Councils, Committees and Boards (6th edition). CBD Research, 1984.

Crawford's Directory of City Connections. Annual, plus regular updates. Crawford's The Economist Publications. (Lists UK quoted and unquoted companies with their financial advisers, auditors, stockbrokers and solicitors. Also covers investment trusts and pension funds.)

Croner's employment law. Looseleaf. Croner.

Croner's reference book for employers. Looseleaf. Croner.

Croner's reference book for exporters. Looseleaf. Croner.

Croner's reference book for importers. Looseleaf. Croner.

Dawson's Little Red Book. Annual. William Dawson and Sons. (Lists over 5000 journal titles alphabetically and also in a classified list by subject.)

Directory of British Associations and Associations in Ireland. Biennial. CBD Research.

Directory of Directors. Annual. Thomas Skinner Directories.

Directory of European industrial and trade associations. CBD Research, 1986.

Directory of European Retailers. Biennial. Newman Books.

Directory of European professional and learned societies. CBD Research, 1988.

Directory of Grant Making Trusts. Biennial. CAF Publications.

Directory of Information Brokers and Consultants. Annual. Information Marketmakers.

Directory of management consultants in the UK. TFPL Publishing, 1988. (Includes library and information consultants.)

Directory of specialist bookdealers in the UK handling mainly new books (3rd edition). P. Marcan, 1985.

Dod's parliamentary companion. Annual. Dod's Parliamentary Companion.

Economist measurement guide and reckoner. Economist Newspaper Ltd, 1980.

Encyclopaedia of consumer credit law. Looseleaf. Sweet and Maxwell.

Europa Yearbook. 2 vols. Annual. Europa Publications.

European Communities Legislation: Current Status. Annual. Butterworth.

EUSIDIC database guide. Learned Information, 1988. (Lists databases available on a worldwide basis.)

Exhibitions and Conferences. Annual. York Publishing Company.

Financial Times Index. Monthly with annual cumulations. Research Publications Ltd.

Fowler's modern English usage (2nd edition). Oxford University Press, 1965, reprinted with corrections 1983.

Good Food Guide. Annual. Hodder and Stoughton.

Good Hotel Guide: Britain and Western Europe. Annual. Consumers Association.

Government Statistics: a Brief Guide to Sources. Annual. Government Statistical Service.

Guide to company information in Great Britain. Longman, 1985.

Guide to Government Department and Other Libraries. Biennial. British Library Science Reference and Information Service.

Guide to Official Statistics. Biennial. HMSO. (A comprehensive guide to tracing sources of official UK statistics.)

Harrap's French/English business dictionary. Harrap, 1986.

Harrap's shorter French/English dictionary (3rd edition). Harrap, 1982.

HMSO in Print on Microfiche. Annual subscription. HMSO.

Industrial Performance and Analysis. Annual. ICC Information Group. (A financial analysis of UK industries and sectors.)

Information Sources Series. (Subjects in separate volumes range from Architecture through Finance to Politics, Science and Technology. An excellent series.) Butterworth.

Inland Revenue Statistics. Annual. HMSO.

Insurance Directory and Yearbook. Annual. Buckley Press.

International Hotel Guide. Annual. International Hotel Association (Paris).

Kelly's Business Directory. Annual. Kelly's Directories. (Both alphabetical and classified listings of companies.)

International Hotel Guide. Annual. International Hotel Association (Paris).

Kompass Register: United Kingdom. 4 vols. Annual. Kompass Publishing Ltd. (Lists over 30,000 companies by name, with detailed cross-referencing by products and services. Also individual volumes for 24 other countries.)

Macmillan encyclopedia (revised edition). Macmillan, 1988.

Major Companies of Europe. Annual. Graham and Trotman.

Management Training Directory. Annual. TFPL Publishing.

Marketsearch: international directory of published market research (12th edition). Arlington Management Ltd, 1988.

Municipal Yearbook and Public Services Directory. Annual. Municipal Publishing Ltd.

Official publications in Britain. Clive Bingley, 1982.

Ordnance Survey Motoring Atlas of Great Britain. 3 miles : 1 inch. Annual. Ordnance Survey and Temple Press.

Oxford dictionary of quotations (3rd edition). Oxford University Press, 1979, reprinted with corrections 1983.

Oxford shorter English dictionary. 2 vols. (3rd edition). Oxford University Press, 1973.

Palmer's company law. 3 vols. (1 bound plus 2 looseleaf). Stevens and Sons.

Public Relations Yearbook. Annual. Financial Times Business Publishing.

Published data on European industrial markets (8th edition). Industrial Aids, 1985.

Publishers in the UK and Their Addresses. Biennial. Whitaker.

Records management directory 1988/89. TFPL Publishing, 1988.

Regional Trends. Annual. HMSO. (Statistical tables.)

Retail Directory. Annual. Newman Books.

Roget's thesaurus (abridged edition). Penguin, 1988.

Royal Institute of Chartered Surveyors Yearbook. Annual. RICS.

Small business guide: sources of information for new and small businesses. British Broadcasting Corporation, 1983.

Social Trends. Annual. HMSO. (Commentary plus tables.)

Solicitors' Diary and Directory. 2 vols. Annual. Waterlow.

Sources of European economic information (5th edition). Gower, 1988

Standard & Poor's Register of Corporations, Directors and Executives. 3 vols. Annual. Standard & Poor. USA.

Statesman's Yearbook. Annual. Macmillan Press.

Stock Exchange admission of securities to listing. Looseleaf. Stock Exchange. (Interpretation of the parts of the Stock Exchange rules and regulations which apply to the listing of companies.)

Stock Exchange Official Yearbook. Annual. Macmillan. (A directory of companies listed on the Stock Exchange and their registrars; also includes a list of companies which ceased to trade during the previous year.)

Sunday Telegraph business finance directory. Graham & Trotman, 1987.

Survey of training materials. Library Association, 1988.

Timetables – international travel timetables and hotel guides are published by ABC International (address in Appendix 3).

Times 1000. Annual. Times Books Ltd. (Lists the 1000 largest UK companies with main financial details, as well as the top trades unions, leading advertisers, city institutions and selected overseas companies.)

Times atlas of the world (7th edition). Times Books, 1987.

Titles and forms of address (18th edition). A & C Black, 1985.

Top 3000 Directories and Annuals. Annual. Alan Armstrong Ltd.

Ulrich's international periodicals directory (26th edition). Bowker, 1987.

UK online search services (3rd edition). Aslib, 1987.

UK Trade Names. Annual. Kompass Publishers.

Vacher's European Companion. Quarterly. A. S. Kerswill.

Vacher's Parliamentary Companion. Quarterly. A. S. Kerswill.

Walford's guide to reference material. 4 vols. Library Association, 1980–1987. (Also available: *Walford's concise guide to reference material*, 1981.)

Whitaker's Almanack. Annual. J. Whitaker and Sons. (A useful general reference book covering countries of the world, as well as giving UK economic and political information.)

Whitaker's Books in Print. Annual. J. Whitaker and Sons. (Also updated monthly on CD-ROM.)

Whitaker's Cumulative Booklist. Annual. J. Whitaker and Sons.

Who Knows: A Guide to Washington Experts (USA). Biennial. Washington Researchers.

Who Owns Whom: Continental Europe. Annual. Dun and Bradstreet.

Who Owns Whom: North America. Annual. Dun and Bradstreet.

Who Owns Whom: UK and Republic of Ireland. 2 vols. Annual and quarterly supplement. Dun and Bradstreet.

Who's Who. Annual. A & C Black.

Willings Press Guide. Annual. Thomas Skinner Directories. (UK and overseas journals listed alphabetically and by subject.)

World Guide to Abbreviations of Organisations (8th edition). Leonard Hill Books, 1987.

World sources of market information. vol 1: Asia/Pacific; vol 2: Africa/Middle East; vol 3: Europe. Gower, 1983.

Writers and Artists Yearbook. Annual A & C Black.

Yearbook of International Associations 1987/88. (24th edition). K. G. Saur, 1988.

Periodicals

Anbar Management Abstracts. 8 times a year. Anbar Publications.

Aslib Information. Monthly. Aslib.

Automation Notes. Monthly. Aslib.

British Business. Weekly. HMSO. (Includes statistical tables.)

British Humanities Index. Monthly. Library Association Publishing.

Business Information Review. Quarterly. Headland Press. (International coverage on the library and information profession in all kinds of library.)

Business Monitor. HMSO. (This is a statistical publication and is produced in various series coded as follows: P for production; SD for service and distribution; M for miscellaneous, followed by A (indicating that it is an annual series), or Q (quarterly), M (monthly), O (occasional, i.e. one-off or at intervals of more than one year), R (repetitive, i.e. at regular intervals of more than one a year but not monthly or quarterly).)

Campaign. Weekly. Marketing Publications Ltd. (Essential source of advertising information. Includes regular surveys on various topics.)

Computer Weekly. Weekly. Reed Business Publishing.

Current Technology Index. Monthly and annual. Library Association Publishing. (An index of technology periodicals.)

Economic Trends. Monthly and Annual. HMSO.

Economist. Weekly. Economist Newspaper Ltd.

Employment Gazette. Monthly. HMSO. (Excellent source of official statistics.)

Estates Gazette. Weekly. Estates Gazette Ltd.

Estates Times. Weekly. Morgan-Grampian Ltd.

Financial Statistics. Monthly. HMSO.

Financial Weekly. Weekly. Pergamon Press.

Fortune. Fortnightly. Time Inc. (International, with emphasis on US business. Includes regular rankings of companies.)

Government Publications. (HMSO produces a daily list of government publications as well as monthly and annual catalogues.)

Incomes Data Services. International reports on pay and conditions of work. Bimonthly. Incomes Data Services.

International Business Week. Weekly. McGraw Hill.

Investors Chronicle. Weekly. Financial Times Business Publishing.

Journal of Business Law. Bimonthly. Stevens and Sons.

Law Society Gazette. Weekly. Law Society.

Library and Information News. Monthly. Alan Armstrong Ltd.

Library Equipment Report. Six times per year. Headland Press.

LISA (Library and Information Science Abstracts). Monthly. Library Association Publishing.

Management Today. Monthly. Management Publications Ltd.

Marketing. Weekly. Marketing Publications Ltd.

Marketing Surveys Index. Monthly. Marketing Surveys Index. (Gives brief abstracts of recent market research reports.)

Money Management. Monthly. FT Business Information Ltd.

New Scientist. Weekly. Holborn Publishing Group

New Society. Weekly. New Science Publications.

Online Notes. Monthly. Aslib.

Online Review. Bimonthly. Learned Information.

Reports Index. Bimonthly. Business Surveys Ltd. (Covers a wide range of reports, including market surveys on various sectors.) Also available online.

Research Index. Fortnightly. Business Surveys Ltd. (A useful index of press articles listed by industry and company name.) Also available online.

Retail Business. Monthly. Economist Intelligence Unit. (Regular reports and surveys of retail products.)

Stock Exchange Daily Official List. Daily. Stock Exchange. (Lists prices of shares quoted on the UK Stock Exchange, including the Unlisted Securities Market.) Available in printed form or on microfiche.

Weekly Information Bulletin. Weekly. HMSO for the House of Commons Public Information Office. (Covers the business of the House of Commons for the past week and forthcoming week; including progress on committees, bills and papers.)

Which? Monthly. Consumers Association.

NB: Indexes, abstracts and in some cases full text articles of journals can be consulted online – see also p. 49.

4 • Physical planning

The physical planning of the library cannot be considered in isolation from the activities of the rest of the organisation. Checklist 1: The organisation (Part 2), in Chapter 1, highlights equipment which can be used by some or all departments, and may or may not be located in the library. Where there is already a library in existence which is being developed in new directions, considerations for physical planning will have been brought out by Checklist 3: Existing library resources, in Chapter 2. This will have indicated furniture and equipment which can be used as it is or successfully adapted to serve another purpose, as well as points about the general environment. The type of service being offered will dictate specific storage requirements according to the format in which information is published, e.g. if newspapers and journals form the basis of the service, you will need to consider storage racks and magazine boxes or microfilm cannisters, microfiche boxes and readers or reader/printers as well as terminals for text-based online services.

In an established business which has decided to set up an information service, it is likely that there will be little choice about the actual amount of space available initially; the librarian's job is to make the best use of it. Given the limitations not only of space, but also of budget, careful planning is vital in the early stages as allowances must be made for growth in the number of items in stock, especially during the first year. Journals will be arriving regularly, and additional items will be purchased as the service becomes operational and the need for further resources becomes apparent. At a later stage extra space may be made available as the service develops and is seen to be a valuable part of the organisation, but, for the moment, planning will be within the constraints mentioned. Any shelving, equipment and furniture must therefore be flexible, adaptable and multi-purpose, as well as contributing to an attractive overall environment in which an effective information service can operate.

The first step is to carry out some careful measuring, with certain questions in mind. Consider the total wall space: how much of it can be used; e.g. could there be shelves from floor to ceiling, what impact do windows, doors, ventilators, radiators, power points, etc. have on the wall span? What is the floor area? Could it accommodate free-standing units; if so how high could they be without impeding the light; would the tops of such units make a useful display area or, if at the right height, a work surface for consulting newspapers, reference books, etc., or act as the base for a card catalogue or microfiche reader? It is important to establish that the load-bearing of the floor is adequate if that part of the building was not originally designed as a library.

Having noted the various measurements of the space available, next calculate the approximate amount and type of storage that will be required for each different sort of material or activity. Think of the number and varying sizes of books and pamphlets; will they be interfiled, how many shelves will be needed, including expansion space; consider the number of journal titles on order (allow for keeping all issues received for at least two years, by which time their usefulness will have been established), and whether they will be displayed as well as filed. Newspapers may be worth filing for a few months or several years, depending on the envisaged use, particularly if complemented by online services. The information needs analysis may have revealed an interest in audiovisual material; how will you store it, will you need space for a projector? If there are to be machines in the library, will their noise level require them to be in a side-room or sound-proof alcove? Is it in fact better not to have the photocopier in the library? It is likely to be used for general copying and the related through-traffic could create a disturbance factor for those studying or researching in the library. This will of course depend on the placing and number of other photocopiers in the building.

Apart from the stock and equipment, space will also be required for library staff and administrative material, e.g. files of correspondence, orders, invoices; various working manuals and office stationery. Study and reading areas must also be included in the planning, and at the same time consideration must be given to general environmental factors such as lighting, heating and ventilation.

Before ordering any equipment or changing anything that is already in place you should undertake the following:

Checklist 5: Physical planning

(1) Familiarise yourself with the recommended basic standards relating to environmental requirements, e.g. level of lighting and heating, ergonomic aspects of seating.

(2) Look carefully at the catalogues of several library suppliers. Most of these are very well produced and give clear and detailed descriptions of everything you will need, from book labels and order pads to

Continued overleaf

Continued from previous page

shelving and workstations. You will also get an idea of how other libraries have been designed from some of the photographs included. Comprehensive collections of such catalogues are maintained by Aslib and by the Library Equipment Centre at the College of Librarianship, Wales, which also acts as a shop window for a number of major suppliers, exhibiting examples of all kinds of library furniture and equipment. In the College library there is a planning collection containing slides, photographs, architects' plans and descriptive material.

(3) Ask what equipment other libraries providing a similar service have found to be useful.

(4) For advice on a particular problem talk to a specialist; either an independent library consultant or the library suppliers themselves, who are often happy to come along and give initial advice free of charge. A number of library and information consultants can be selected from the appropriate directories in the core list; others can be contacted through Aslib and the Library Association. The Royal Institute of British Architects offers a service which will help any company or firm concerned with information relating to the construction industry to set up a library, whether they are building firms, architectural practices, chartered surveyors or any other interested organisation. The Library Equipment Centre (mentioned under section 2) also answers postal and telephone enquiries.

(5) For detailed information on specific aspects of physical planning read one of the more specialised texts or journals and see the appropriate section in the list of further reading.

(6) Check to see if any suitable equipment or furniture is available in-house.

Having established what is required and what is already available in the building, draw up several plans of possible layout, incorporating the various features required to give the sort of service envisaged and to make the most efficient use of space. There is such a wide range of library equipment on offer at varying prices that it should not be difficult to put together an arrangement which is both practical and attractive. For example, metal shelving comes in various colours; it can be combined with timber, say in the form of end panels, which can in turn be matched to other furniture in the library, such as desks, tables and chairs. Pamphlet boxes are produced in a number of materials and colours, making it possible to co-ordinate them into the overall design. Some

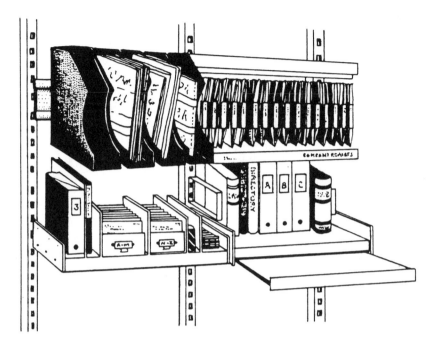

Multi-purpose shelf unit

shelving systems have interchangeable components so that items such as books, audiovisual material and subject files can all be housed together in one unit, which may also incorporate storage cupboards or pull-out desk shelves.

Storage capacity can be greatly increased by using rolling bookshelf systems such as Compactus, where bookcases have no aisles between them, but are moved as access is required. However, despite the advantage of space creation, it is not suitable for many small libraries, where most of the stock is being consulted regularly, as it allows access to only one section at a time. It is therefore more suitable for material which is not frequently consulted. Because of the density of storage it is very heavy and also requires rolling equipment to be set into the floor. One exception is Templestock's Supreme ThinLine Rollaway which offers the benefit of increased storage capacity without the need for tracks to be fixed in the floor. Instead these are part of a common base which can be moved and added to as required. Templestock also offers a design and consultancy service. Their address is in Appendix 4.

It is important that all shelving is adjustable and each shelf deep enough to cater for a variety of size and format of material, and for future changes in arrangement. It is practical to choose a standard design where it will be easy to add further components and buy ancillary items, such as shelf dividers or end supports, at a later date.

Rotary stand

If journal display is required, a rotary stand takes little floor space and offers the facility to store approximately four to six journals behind the current copy.

If more storage space is required, the rotary stand can be used in conjunction with magazine boxes or cupboards; alternatively, a straight stand with sloping lift-up shelves will provide both display and storage space. As well as the rotary journal stand illustrated, which is available from Gresswell, there is another excellent range from Templestock. Their circular filing stand, Rotatrieve, offers high-density storage for files. Books and bulkier items will fit well on Templestock's ThinLine range.

If no display is required, journals can be filed in an open storage rack, or in magazine boxes arranged alphabetically by title on shelves, or they can be organised in hanging files or boxes. These are also useful for subject files, pamphlet collections where pamphlets are not interfiled with the book stock, and reports.

Library suppliers' catalogues will give you a good idea of the range of possibilities for incorporating study facilities into the plan, with such choices as tables, divided desks, and study carrels. Appropriate seating must also be looked at.

Administrative material and stationery can be organised in a variety of ways depending on format and frequency of use. It is best to keep items required

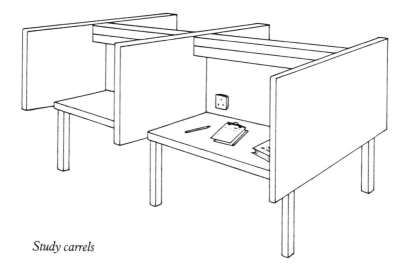

Study carrels

regularly, e.g. order forms and standard letters, in an open box file or expanding file on a stand which brings it up to desk height for ease of use, if the desk itself does not contain any deep filing drawers. The masters can be stored on the word processor or computer, or in printed form.

Filing cabinets, hanging files or box files can be used for organising correspondence, invoices and publishers' catalogues. If box files are used, these will require some shelf space, as will larger stationery items such as padded bags for posting books, boxes of cards, and supplies of internal distribution envelopes. A locking desk or cupboard is advisable for the security not only of personal valuables, but also for such things as calculators, the control units of equipment, and confidential or restricted circulation material.

In addition to the various units and other forms of storage available, consideration must be given to the user aspects of physical planning, i.e. there should be clear labelling of shelves, files and boxes; clear instructions on equipment; shelf guides and book supports should be movable so that they can be moved with the stock; supports across the backs of shelves will prevent items falling down behind the units; boxes and files should not be over-filled, making them difficult to handle; heavy or large books should not be placed on very high or very low shelves and ideally should be in a unit incorporating a desk shelf for study purposes; high shelves should be reserved for less regularly used stock, and library steps should be available; an adjustable-height chair may be required for use with keyboard facilities, e.g. computer terminal 'or word processor; potted plants or display material on top of lower bookcases can create the illusion of alcoves for reading or studying. The whole environment should be attractive to the user and the physical arrangement of the material must contribute to its maximum effectiveness.

Checklist 6: Typical stock and equipment to be considered when planning a library

(1) Equipment
Typewriter
Word processor
Computer terminal and screen
Modem
Keyboard
Telephone
Telex station
Facsimile transmission equipment
Television set
Video recording equipment
Cassette player
Headphones
Audiovisual units
Projectors
Screens
Photocopier
Microfilm reader/printer
Microfiche reader/printer
Portable desklights
Portable heaters and electric fans
Power points

(2) Furniture
Desks
Workstation units
Chairs
Typist's chair
Filing cabinet
Small filing system, e.g.
    expanding file
Locking cupboard
Shelves for administrative
    material
Work table (i.e. for display
    work, book processing,
    etc.)
Study tables and chairs
Study carrels
Pull-out desk shelves
Catalogue

(3) Stock	**Possible storage method**
Books and looseleaf services	Shelves
Pamphlets	Shelves, pamphlet boxes, hanging files
Journals	Magazine boxes, hanging files, display stands, cupboards, microfilm or fiche
Newspapers	Shelves, racks, boxes, cupboards, microfilm or fiche
Reports	Pamphlet boxes, hanging files
Maps, plans	Large vertical files or shallow drawers – both accommodated in metal or wooden cabinets

Cassettes	Plastic storage trays or boxes with dustproof lids	
Tapes	Shallow plastic or metal cannisters	
Slides	Plastic storage boxes or trays; plastic sleeves with compartments for individual slides – these are available in binders or for use in suspension files.	In addition there are a number of specially designed storage units for audiovisual materials in the Don Gresswell catalogue
Overhead projector transparencies	Flat storage boxes	
Film reels	Metal cannisters in boxes stored vertically on shelves	
Film cartridges	Boxes in drawers or on shelves	
Microfilm	Metal cannisters in a drawer cabinet	
Microfiche	In panels which fit into a binder or on to a rotating stand, or in acid-free envelopes in drawers	
Cuttings	Cardboard wallets in box files or hanging files	
Discs	For wordprocessors or computers; always keep dust-free in paper covers in permanent storage boxes; keep away from extremes of temperature and large-scale electrical machinery, including trains, trams and trolley-buses, otherwise you risk losing the stored information	
Administrative and other documents	Ring binders; folders in box files with an internal spring clip or in a filing cabinet; word processor or computer files	

Further reading

DOIDGE, R. Physical arrangement and display, circulation and loan. In: L. J. Anthony (ed.). *Handbook of special librarianship and information work* (5th edition). London: Aslib, 1982.

RITCHIE, Sheila. *Modern library practice* (2nd edition). Buckden: ELM Publications, 1982. (Chapter 10 gives detailed coverage of physical planning.)

SCHMIDT, Janet. *Marketing the modern information center*. New York: FIND/SVP, 1987. (Chapter 6 covers public relations and promotion, including signs, physical layout and floorplans.)

5 • *Making the most of technology*

(Note: specific brands of equipment and software have not been cited as this is a field of rapid change. Sources to consult are suggested in the checklist and appendices.)

The last thing you want is a computer! No, not heresy, nor a rejection of technology, but an important reminder that when you are considering the potential of the computer in your new service, the first decision to be taken concerns what you want to achieve through its use. Technology, when selected and used appropriately, can bring a whole range of benefits in terms of the breadth of service which can be offered and the facility to develop efficient and cost-effective procedures through which to offer it. But that initial selection is important, particularly when the costs form part of that valuable first budget.

Therefore, look first at the areas in which computer applications would offer maximum effectiveness, secondly at the software that would allow you to carry out those activities, thirdly consider the storage implications, and only then look at the computer, or hardware, itself. If you have not had a great deal of practical experience in using computers, now is the time to do some homework, familiarising yourself with library applications and with the basic terminology surrounding them. Some introductory reading, such as that suggested at the end of the chapter, supported by discussions with colleagues in similar organisations, will provide a very valuable starting point. Particularly helpful is *The librarian's guide to microcomputers for information management*, which uses definitions and simple explanations throughout. Comment on more general considerations of using information technology, putting it into a broader organisational perspective, will be found in *Strategic control of information technology*, one of a series of useful introductory booklets published by the Chartered Institute of Management Accountants. TFPL Ltd runs a two-day course which considers the decisions involved in deciding what to computerise and how to set about it. Details of the course, 'So you want to computerise?', can be obtained from TFPL at the address given in Appendix 2.

Other ways of finding out about the types and uses of information technology are listed below.

Checklist 7: How to find out about information technology

(1) Discuss with other users in similar organisations
(2) Carry out relevant reading (books, journals, trade literature)
(3) Visit suppliers and dealers
(4) Go to exhibitions and demonstrations
(5) Attend short courses and seminars (regularly announced in journals listed at the end of chapter)
(6) Consult
    — professional associations
    — special interest groups
    — training organisations
    — specialist centres (see Appendices)
    — relevant academic departments
    — database producers and hosts
    — information consultants

The Aslib Information Resources Centre (IRC) maintains a databank of Aslib members willing to discuss their uses of IT with other members. The databank contains details of software and hardware used for library automation purposes as well as for internal databases. It also provides details of online databases and hosts accessed by members and the equipment used. Other aspects of IT such as the use of electronic mail, facsimile transmission and CD-ROM, are included. The information is supplied in confidence and will therefore be searched by Aslib IRC staff on behalf of enquirers.

The success or failure of the new service will depend, among other things, on the degree of care with which the selection and balancing of resources is carried out in this early stage. If you are intending to set up any sort of internal database, from a full catalogue to a list of working papers, with appropriate cross-referencing, as well as using the computer for administrative procedures and online searching, you will need adequate storage capacity.

It seems to be common practice in business to expect a minimum working life of about three years from the equipment, if not more, before it is replaced or upgraded, so you will certainly need to have worked out carefully all the possible requirements for that time span. It is no good finding one year later that your chosen configuration or set-up cannot cope with your planned developments, thereby limiting the range of services that you had hoped to offer.

However, organisational policy may dictate standardisation, i.e. the requirement to conform with the system already in operation. This could mean linking in to the existing mainframe system or, if microcomputers are widely used throughout the organisation, buying additional microcomputers of the same make. In either case do check that the software which suits your specialist requirements is compatible with the particular type of machine in use. It may be that even if a particular system is used in other departments there will be no problem in buying a different make of machine, as long as it can be justified as being the most appropriate to the new service. Having said that, most current software and machines, particularly microcomputers, are much more flexible and interchangeable than ever before and are likely to become increasingly more so, particularly with the use of expert systems packages. These are proving to be highly suited to the training field because of their interactive nature, which also offers great potential for library applications. Developments in the latter area are regularly discussed in the journal *Expert Systems for Information Management*.

Having followed through Checklist 1, Part 2 and Checklist 3 you will already be familiar with what exists in terms of equipment. Your information needs analysis will have determined the kind of information provision which the organisation requires. It is now a case of co-ordinating these details in order to be able to make the best use of the computer as a resource. The computer can help you make the most effective use of your time and skills, as well as allowing you instant access to an enormous range of information resources which you could never hope to have in-house. Not only that, but it will also allow you to do things with the information which would just not otherwise be possible, or would be a very cumbersome procedure if they were possible manually.

What can the computer do for you? That is your choice. It need not just act as a means of automating formerly manual procedures, or of merely storing information previously kept in traditional printed form. Of course, it does both those things, but it can also calculate and manipulate the data that it is handling. It allows the editing and updating of text, assists in detailed planning, enhances procedures and offers the facility to add value to raw data and to present the final outcome in a well-structured way. In combination with telecommunications facilities it allows access to, and transmission of, information worldwide.

Perhaps at this point we should consider some of the areas in which the computer can help you, both in the early stages of setting up a library and information service, and in its later development. These could be divided into broad groups according to the types of task which could be made easier or more effective by the use of a computer, e.g. information retrieval, database management or data communications. They could also involve the use of word processing and spreadsheets. All these will facilitate the organisation and exploitation of information which is held or generated internally, as well as providing a means of external communication with users or databases. In the setting-up situation it is better to plan realistic objectives, rather than attempt everything at once and perhaps achieve little to your satisfaction. Take your computer applications in stages, along with your other developments, particularly if they are likely to require a large amount of data input. If you are a one-person unit, or have little assistance, you will be anxious to get the service off the ground. Your potential users will be looking for early results, so your choice of which computer application to move into first will be an important one.

Accessing online databases

When setting up a new service, as well as planning the means of providing information, you are seeking to develop a presence. This is likely to be best achieved by being able to respond to requests for information at the earliest possible stage. It could therefore be most appropriate to use the computer first to access online databases. This is particularly relevant where the information required is clearly defined and falls into a specific category. I have come across several examples among stockbroking firms and banks where this has been the case. The information needs analysis revealed that the main requirement was for financial and economic data, both real-time and historic. This was an area already well-served by commercially available databases and thus allowed the services a rapid take-off. In all cases there was also a need for general information which was met by adding a basic reference collection selected from the core list given in Chapter 3.

In other subject fields the information needs may not be as specific, and may not be as comprehensively covered by the use of a distinct group of databases. What may be required instead could be regular but less frequent use of each of a broad spectrum of databases covering a range of subject areas. For example, in the library of a large pharmaceutical company there is likely to be as much need for information on markets and competititors' activities as on scientific matters. When setting up a broad-based service it is therefore crucial to ensure that the mix is right.

You will need to start asking questions such as the following:

— Is all the information required available online?
— If not, what other sources will provide the balance?

Then move on to more specific questions relating to the number and location of access points, e.g.:

— Will databases be searched by the end-user or by an intermediary, e.g. the librarian, researcher or information officer?
— Where will such searching take place, e.g. in the information centre or at the individual manager's desk?
— How many terminals will be required to allow both scientists and business managers to satisfy their information needs simultaneously?

You will have other questions to add to these, according to the environment in which you are operating.

Somewhere in between these two examples of the small or medium-sized specific service and the large broad-based one, there will be a number of you setting up a small unit needing to be able to supply 'instant information' on a range of topics. And you and your staff will be carrying out most, if not all, of the searching. The above questions and others which follow, need to be addressed whatever the size and subject interests of the organisation.

How can you establish what is available and evaluate the usefulness of the numerous databases now on the market? Checklist 7 will help you to answer the first part of the question and go some way towards making a start on evaluation, particularly through hearing about other users' experiences of, and views on, certain databases. On the basis of your earlier finding-out exercise you will be able to make an initial selection of those databases which look to be most useful to you. The Cuadra *Directory of Online Databases* is an excellent comprehensive list of the databases available and what they cover. Checklist 8 lists the criteria by which you can begin to evaluate them.

Checklist 8: Online databases – evaluation criteria

(1) Coverage
— by subject
— by time span (historic and current)
(2) Reliability
— accuracy and authority of data
— technically dependable
(3) Speed of retrieval
(4) Relevance of output
(5) Overlap with other databases
(6) Ease of use
(7) Potential frequency of use
(8) Support and backup from producer (quality of documentation, help desk)
(9) Cost and method of payment

By testing each database in these terms you will get a clearer picture of how you will be able to best build up your total information resource to match the needs expressed in your earlier information needs analysis.

If you are intending to access a number of databases using different command languages, then search strategy and training are all important. All the time that you spend online means money spent online. Well-trained searchers know which databases to search and how to get the best out of them. Initial training is offered by most database producers and hosts, with some providing this on site for individual companies. In addition, professional associations, special interest and user groups, as well as training organisations, arrange meetings, seminars and courses. A selection of those located in the United Kingdom are indicated in the appendices. For other countries it would be best to start by consulting the national associations listed in the *International guide to library, archival and information science associations*. They would be able to advise on what is available both nationally and regionally in each country. You should also scan the columns of the various online journals in which current courses, conferences and exhibitions will be advertised. Three practical papers on training online searchers can be found in *Information online 86*, the proceedings of the First Australian Online Information Conference.

You may want to have the option to choose from a variety of databases whilst maintaining a simple search mechanism. Here the intelligent gateway could be the answer. At the time of writing, those operating vary considerably in terms of speed and cost, but are rapidly improving and will provide an efficient means of access, whether by the end-user or the information intermediary, to a wide range of databases. Easynet, well-established in the USA, is just one example of an intelligent gateway which has been well-received by both categories of user. One end-user view is put forward by Gitte Larsen, who, in summarising the results of testing and evaluating Easynet, points out that it can be as valuable to the experienced searcher as to the untrained user. However experienced the searcher, he or she is still likely to use some databases less frequently than others and will also need to learn about new ones. In such cases the intelligent gateway can provide a very useful short cut. In the United Kingdom, Istel Infosearch now provides links into Easynet as well as access to other database hosts directly through its own networks. It is likely that during your online searching you will come across information which you would like to store for future reference. You could of course just store the printout, but a far less cumbersome process would be to download the search, or part of it, i.e. transferring the information from the online database directly to a disc for storage. It could then be retrieved as required either as it stands or as an integrated part of any internal database which you may create. It is important to check with each database producer whether downloading is permitted. The legal implications of downloading are described in Chapter 15 of *Online information: a comprehensive business-user's guide*, which also includes a glossary of technical terms.

The setting-up of any internal database will play an important part in ensuring that best use is made of all your information resources, in whatever format they exist. This is discussed in the section on collection management.

CD-ROM

An increasing number of information sources are being produced in CD-ROM format (compact disc-read only memory). At the time of writing these fall into four main groups:

1. bibliographic – either broad-ranging, such as Bookbank published by J. Whitaker & Sons, or specific, like the index to Legal Periodicals from H.W. Wilson & Co.
2. company/financial – such as that produced by Disclosure
3. reference books – complete works ranging from the McGraw-Hill Science & Technology Set to the Luther Bible or a dictionary of medical terms in Spanish
4. demographic – ranging from census material to post codes and addresses

There are other miscellaneous products which do not fall into the above categories, covering, for example, business information, telephone numbers, airline statistics. A growing awareness of the potential of CD-ROM is being expressed by the education sector with products already available giving information on courses, as well as bibliographical information and reference works. Details of all these are given in the *CD-ROM Directory* which is published annually. It has international coverage and not only includes details of the products and their producers, but also lists related books, journals, conferences and exhibitions.

Collection management

You may have been appointed to your present post primarily to reorganise and further develop existing resources. This could involve drawing together a number of scattered collections, or co-ordinating internally and externally generated information into a new central service. It could mean operating a complete records management service, including correspondence control, archives and reprographics services. An impressive example of just such a comprehensive approach is that developed at Woodside Petroleum's Perth office, which I visited in Australia. This is described in *Approaches to business information in Australia and the United Kingdom*. Although this example is drawn from the world of business, the application could be equally relevant in other organisational settings.

Effective collection management entails a different approach to that of online searching. Rather than simply retrieving information from a specific database, you will be using the computer as a means of organising and managing information for its more effective use. For example, you may want to use the computer to make a central listing of all resources, even if they are not going to be located centrally. This is particularly helpful when the aim is to make better use of internal documents, such as working papers, client proposals and reports, emanating from different departments but of potential value across several of them.

As well as setting up a catalogue of the stock, you may wish to have a series of cross-references from your internal resources to known external sources of information in the same subject area. Where the collection consists mainly of non-book material, e.g. training films, trade literature and software packages, it could be useful to refer to relevant databases or printed sources which would supply valuable complementary information as and when required. An index to enquiries can also be extremely useful in avoiding duplication of effort and in saving time. It provides a base of information which only needs to be updated when required, rather than having to be sought in its entirety each time there is a request in that subject field. It is in these applications that you will need to consider how it will be best to cross-refer. You could build on the classification scheme already in use, or construct a thesaurus or a simple key word index. If no such schemes are in use, perhaps one of those which you have seen elsewhere can be used as it stands or with slight modifications (see Chapter 9, on classification).

Database management packages will make the task easy once you have decided which approach you want to take. The software is improving all the time and there are now some very easy-to-use relational database packages which produce excellent results. These packages allow you to index and subsequently search by different aspects (known as fields) of the material being put into the database. Take, for example, a collection of company documents such as annual accounts, takeover circulars, share options schemes. Your organisation may have regular requirements to search a range of documents by various criteria, all of which may not be covered by commercially available online databases. Here the facility to be able to build up a tailor-made searchable database is invaluable. Database management packages allow you to index by whatever fields you choose, using whatever source material you wish to include, thus building up a powerful database tailored to your requirements. Dixon and Rawlings' *Introduction to database systems* offers in 29 pages a simple explanation of the concept of database management.

As mentioned elsewhere, the experience of others can be very helpful both in your choice of approach and in the selection of software. Refer to Checklist 8 again – it is equally valid when seeking to find out about software packages. Burton and Petrie offer further considerations in their checklist on software assessment. One useful starting point, which indicates what packages exist and what they can do in this and other areas, is the directory produced by the Institute of Information Scientists.

Collection management means managing the total information resource to maximise its usefulness. Often the value of the information will be directly related to the speed with which it can be supplied and the format in which it is presented. Here is a simple example showing the comparison of companies in a given sector, as produced by using a spreadsheet package.

Spreadsheet example: Percentage of turnover by activity

Co. name	Retailing Outlets				Distribution	
	Super-markets	Chains	Dept stores	Franchise outlets	Bulk	Direct
ABC LTD	60.0%	14.0%	0.0%	0.0%	20.0%	6.0%
W & CO.	0.0%	0.0%	0.0%	74.0%	26.0%	0.0%
XCO LTD	0.0%	23.0%	66.0%	0.0%	11.0%	0.0%
YNOT CO.	68.0%	10.0%	0.0%	0.0%	24.0%	8.0%
ZED LTD	72.0%	0.0%	10.0%	0.0%	18.0%	0.0%
Average %	40.0%	9.4%	15.2%	14.8%	19.8%	2.8%

Not only does the above example set out information clearly, it also suggests to the enquirer a structured and professional approach by the information staff, as well as proficiency in the use of computers.

Any report or analysis is best presented in typed or printed form. It will be prepared most easily either by the use of a spreadsheet as indicated, or a word processing package, depending on the format desired, e.g. columns or paragraphs, and whether calculation or text manipulation facilities are required. This is discussed further in the next section. For the moment let us return to the process of presenting and passing on the information.

The degree of acceptance and use of office automation within the organisation will dictate how much use you can make of technology in passing on information and in what format it needs to be prepared. For example, facsimile transmission (fax) is an extremely convenient means of sending information from one place to another, either nationally or internationally. To make the most cost-effective use of fax, the subject matter must be clearly set out, making maximum use of each sheet to be transmitted; therefore typescript or a clear photocopy of printed material is preferable.

Not only do telecommunications play a vital part in sending information, but also, given the appropriate model of telephone, they can provide direct access to certain external databases such as Dunsvoice, without any add-on computer facility being required at the user end. Instead, the press-buttons are used to interrogate the database. Telephones also allow multi-user discussion, which can be very valuable to those engaged in a meeting who may suddenly have urgent need of particular information. They will be able to call the information centre and discuss their requirement as a group, clarifying as they go along. That is just a simple example. Electronic mail, or e-mail, as it is commonly known, is another extremely appropriate means of relaying requests for information and the resultant responses. E-mail saves time in that the call can be made whether or not the intended recipient is at the other end, therefore no repeat calls are necessary in order to relay the message. The total message, perhaps a lengthy report, can be prepared in advance before you call up the e-mail number, thus saving considerable connect time. E-mail also allows access via gateways to various external databases, offers a telex facility, and bulletin boards for announcements, the latter often operating on a closed user group basis. If you are not a subscriber to an e-mail service it is worth finding out what facilities the in-house word processing system offers, e.g. to be able to transmit a telex direct from your workstation rather than having to go to a central telex machine. Office automation facilities of the kind just described are continually being improved, and new services introduced. They certainly make the job of passing on information a smoother one, as well as offering considerable savings in time and money.

Departmental organisation and planning

As well as organising the resource from which the information needs of other people will be met, you will also have an information management need yourself for which you will have to cater. There will be various tasks such as budgeting, charging and staff planning, which involve the regular collection and analysis of certain data. Wherever you require figures or other data to be shown in columns, or where you need a calculating facility, use a spreadsheet package. It is simple to use, will enable you to present information clearly for reporting purposes, and act as a time-saving management tool. As was illustrated in the previous section, the spreadsheet provides an excellent means of presenting certain types of research results for an enquirer. It could be used just as easily for setting out an analysis of enquiries over a certain period of time, on which to base future staff or information resources planning. For example, the increase in enquiry work could be set out to illustrate the need for additional staff or to show the type of work which could be built up as an income generator if a large proportion of the work is external. Further analysis could include a costing of the staff time involved, also the types of information resource used to achieve successful results and the comparative costs of purchasing them versus using an external agency.

In using the computer as a management aid, whether for collection management or for departmental planning, what you will have to do first is to decide on the types of record that you will need to keep; also give consideration to the related updating and analysis that you and the organisation will require for both day-to-day and longer-term planning. Examples could include the recording of staff time for scheduling and charging purposes; job rotas; training schedules; enquiry statistics; and budget details. User surveys and information needs analyses are other areas which could benefit from being handled by the computer.

It should be noted that in many countries there is a requirement to observe data protection legislation when personal data is stored in computer form. In the United Kingdom this is expressed in the Data Protection Act 1984. The implications for the UK library and information profession are comprehensively covered by J. Eric Davies in his book on the subject. Legislation outside the United Kingdom, often referred to as privacy legislation, is well-summarised in John Martyn's article 'Data Protection legislation outside the UK'.

There will also be various housekeeping tasks with which the computer can help, for example in ordering and payment procedures and in the distribution and circulation of material. In the latter case, not only will the computer maintain the lists of items and names, but it will also be able to print out internal circulation slips as well as labels for external distribution. For this you can use special purpose software or the facilities which exist within most word processing packages, although the latter may be somewhat limited depending on your particular requirement. Word processing packages will also allow you to set up a standard format for the production of regular newsletters and bulletins; to compile reading lists which will be able to be updated as required; to put together standard letters, the paragraphs of which can be easily interchanged; and to design and store the masters for various pieces of internal stationery, which can then be printed out and reproduced when stocks are needed. All these documents can be edited whenever necessary, making it a very efficient way of handling the process. The manual of procedures, your key to day-to-day operations (see Chapter 6), lends itself particularly well to such treatment. Sections can be updated as procedures are changed, and amended sheets produced for inclusion in the hard copy file.

Promoting and publicising the service, ensuring that others are kept up-to-date with changes and new developments, is as much part of departmental planning as it is of collection management. Everything that you do, whether it involves preparing a report, designing a form, or passing on the response to an enquiry, conveys a message about you and the service. The computer can provide considerable help in this. You must learn to make the best use of it, whilst not losing sight of the importance of other factors, such as subject knowledge, management and interpersonal skills, in creating an information service. Manual procedures are described throughout this book. However, these often exist side-by-side, or are developed in conjunction with information technology. For example, where the emphasis is on online searching there is still likely to be a book collection, however small. In this case it may be more cost-effective and user-friendly to have a small card catalogue rather than one in computer form. The card catalogue is quick and easy to search, requires no power or telecommunications back-up, and no more keyboard input than the computer. On the other hand, where there is a terminal on every desk, or in each department, even a small collection could merit an automated catalogue, allowing instant reference for users, without the need to physically visit the library or information unit. Not only could they consult the catalogue, but also place requests and receive the response via the terminal.

The use of the computer does not necessarily preclude the use of manual procedures. Both have their place; you must choose which is the most appropriate for each purpose, given the specific environment in which you are establishing your service. Throughout Europe, North America, and the developed countries generally, there is a rich choice of both hardware and software. However, the availability in some developing countries will vary considerably for social, economic and political reasons. This is well-demonstrated by Dr Muhammad A. Marghalani in his article 'Factors affecting information technology transfer in developing countries', in which he also puts forward suggestions for solving some of the problems.

Further reading

Automation Notes. London: Aslib, monthly.

BENTLEY, T.J. *Strategic control of information technology*. London: Chartered Institute of Management Accountants, 1988.

BURTON, P.F. and PETRIE, J.H. *The librarian's guide to microcomputers for information management* (2nd edition). Wokingham: Van Nostrand Reinhold (UK) Ltd, 1986.

CD-ROM Directory. London: TFPL Publishing, annual.

DAVIES, J.E. *Data protection: a guide for library and information management*. London: Elsevier International Bulletins, 1984.

Directory of Online Databases. New York: Cuadra/Elsevier, quarterly.

DIXON, R., *Expert systems in context*. London: Chartered Institute of Management Accountants, 1988.

DIXON, R. and RAWLINGS, G. *Introduction to database systems*. London: Chartered Institute of Management Accountants, 1988.

Expert Systems for Information Management. London: Taylor Graham, three times a year.

FIDEL, R. *Database design for information retrieval*. New York: Wiley, 1987.

Information online 86. Proceedings of the First Australian Online Information Conference held at Sydney, 20 – 22 January 1986, 77 – 106. Sydney: Library Association of Australia, 1986.

International guide to library, archival and information science associations (2nd edition). New York and London: Bowker, 1980.

KIMBERLEY, Robert. *Text retrieval: a directory of software*. Aldershot: Gower in conjunction with the Institute of Information Scientists, 1987. (Looseleaf with 3 updates per annum.)

LARSEN, G. Searching the intelligent gateway Easynet – the end-user's point of view. *The Electronic Library*, Vol. 5, No. 3, June 1987, 146–151.

MARGHALANI, Dr Muhammad A. Factors affecting information technology transfer in developing countries. *Aslib Proceedings*, Vol. 39, No. 11/12, November/December 1987, 355–359.

MARTYN, JOHN. Data protection legislation outside the UK. *Aslib Proceedings*, Vol. 37, No. 8, August 1985, 329–337.

TEDD, L.A. Progress in documentation. Computer-based library systems: a review of the last twenty-one years. *Journal of Documentation*, Vol. 43, No. 2, June 1987. 145–165. (A very useful discussion of the various types of library application.)

TURPIE, G. *Going online 1988*. London: Aslib, 1988.

WALSH, B.P., BUTCHER, H. and FREUND, A. *Online information: a comprehensive business-user's guide*. Oxford: Basil Blackwell, 1987.

WEBB, S.P. Approaches to business information in Australia and the United Kingdom. *Business Information Review*, Vol. 4, No. 1, July 1987, 29–34.

6 • *Procedures and records: what is required?*

Administrative procedures and records are viewed by some as necessary evils to be put to one side for as long as possible. Why not reverse that and set them up so that they work for you? They can then be seen as positive assets and provide ways of finding required information in the shortest possible time. They are your means of cutting through the necessary and ongoing administration which accompanies the setting up and running of an information service.

There are two basic rules to be observed when setting up procedures. The first is to keep a written note of each procedure for future reference; and the second is to keep all procedures simple. Simplicity is most important from the point of view of the initial time and effort involved in setting up the procedure, and that involved in its ongoing use. It will also enable future modifications to take place easily as the service develops and changes are required. This is where technology can prove its worth, as discussed in the previous chapter.

To return to the first rule, that of keeping a written note, this will serve a number of purposes. First, it records your decision on the perceived most appropriate way of carrying out a task which is likely to occur on a regular basis. This means that until that procedure becomes second nature, you will not have to re-think it each time it arises. These written summaries will grow in number, and can be organised to serve a second purpose, that of a manual of procedures or staff manual. Although you may develop the manual by using your computer, a printed version still provides a handy desk reference tool.

These manuals have a number of uses. They serve the first purpose mentioned, that of providing a source of reference until the use of a procedure becomes established; they are extremely valuable in training additional staff, or for temporary staff to turn to in the absence of the librarian; they provide an excellent starting point for the librarian's successor, if the librarian takes up another appointment; they can be used as the basis for an annual review of the service; and they provide information on which to draw when writing memoranda concerning the library and how it works, e.g. notes to new members of staff as they join the organisation, as well as in the preparation of library presentations, guides and notices.

The following are the types of procedures and notes that could usefully make up such a manual. Wherever a printed document or the layout of material is described, examples and illustrations provide valuable clarification and should be filed with the appropriate note.

Checklist 9: What to include in a manual of procedures

(N.B. Specific procedures are described in more detail in the appropriate chapters.)

(1) *Administrative details general to the organisation*
— For example stationery (where and when it can be obtained), photocopying, typewriter repairs, fire drill, etc. Such details may be available as a general staff booklet and can be filed in that form.

(2) *Outline and description of the library service*
— includes details of the type of stock and services provided and the criteria for them; shows where the library fits into the organisation and its links with other departments; includes examples of any library guides, bulletins, newsletters and specialised stationery, e.g. enquiry forms, with notes on their use.

(3) *Daily routines*
— what they are and the preferred method of handling, e.g. post, starting up and shutting down of equipment, security aspects such as window-closing, locking up, etc. Certain daily routines will need to be cross-referenced to other sections of the manual, e.g. circulation and distribution of material; receipt and marking-in procedures.

(4) *Budget*
— how administered; records required, any changes made.

(5) *Selection of stock* (see Chapter 7)

(6) *Order and receipt of books and journals*
This will include a list of which suppliers to use for various types of material; an example of the order form used and the numbers of copies required for filing; a printout of the format if the process is computerised; the arrangement of copy orders, e.g. by title, author, supplier, date, etc.; follow-up procedure where orders have not been received; marking-in of orders on receipt; checking of invoices; allocation of accession numbers if used; checking if the item has been requested by a particular person or not and processing it accordingly.

Continued overleaf

Continued from previous page

(7) *Invoices and payments*
  — dates on which the organisation usually pays invoices, e.g. end- of-month
  — how many signatures, and whose, are required
  — nominal ledger codes used to differentiate payments, e.g.
    301 = books for library stock
    302 = material for other departments
    303 = journals
    304 = online services, etc.
  — petty cash arrangements
  — records required, e.g. copy invoices.

(8) *Correspondence files*
  — order of filing, e.g. by date; company; individual name, etc.
  — number of copies required
  — how long correspondence is kept
  — standard letters
  — logging or progressing procedures if word processing is used.

(9) *Classification and cataloguing*
  This will outline the classification scheme, or other method of stock arrangement in use, as well as stating preferred ways of handling cataloguing for your particular library's requirements.

(10) *Processing of stock*
  — includes accessioning; identifying, i.e. with a mark of ownership; labelling; putting on plastic book jacket covers; adding book pockets, date labels as required, according to the loan system in use; special treatment for any particular type of material.

(11) *Loan and circulation system*
  — including examples of any forms or cards used; interlibrary loans.

(12) *Looseleaf services*
  — any special procedures which may be unusual or specific to a particular publication.

(13) *Books, journals, newspapers*
  — includes notes on the length of time for which journals and newspapers are kept. Alternatively this can be shown on the visible index, the computer record, or in the card catalogue and merely referred to on the note.
  — policy on binding, microfilming, etc.
  — notes of any items regularly passed on to other departments or libraries when no longer current, e.g. previous issues of reference books as well as periodicals; stock check or review procedures.

(14) *Subject files*
  — criteria for inclusion of material.

(15) *Other information services used*
   — for example press cuttings and card services, microfiche, microfilm, online, plus contact names for all services.

(16) *External resources*
   — reciprocal arrangements with other libraries, e.g. exchange of publications. (A list of regularly-used contacts in other libraries is best kept as a card index to which new cards can easily be added, or as a computer file.)
   — membership of organisations and groups, e.g. Aslib
   — no-cost material, i.e. material produced regularly by organisations, e.g. bank reviews, statistical summaries, etc.

(17) *Publications produced by the organisation*
   — includes printing arrangements and distribution.

As well as including notes of procedures, the manuals can be expanded to include lists of various suppliers who may have been approached, with comments on their services (criteria for choosing a book supplier will be given in Chapter 8); library progress reports; papers of presentations made with copies of any supporting material used, e.g. visual aids; the reports on visits to other libraries; comments on any courses attended by library staff; as well as various notes on organisational and library policy.

This then becomes more of a general library manual rather than just a manual of procedures. Either way, i.e. one general manual, or separate manuals for the various areas covered, the arrangement of the material is important. The easiest method for a printed manual is to write a keyword in bold letters on the top right-hand corner of each item to be filed e.g. JOURNALS, and to file by keyword in alphabetical order. This ensures easy retrieval and continuous expansion. As with other systems of filing, cross-references can be used where there is a choice of term, e.g. if there is material concerning the production of internal publications it may include information on printing. The material could be filed under PUBLICATIONS, and a plain sheet of paper headed PRINTING *see* PUBLICATIONS could be filed under PRINTING. The same keywords can be used in a computerised version.

The very nature of a manual is that it is never complete, its value lies in the fact that it is ongoing, constantly changing, and always up-to-date. This last point is particularly important if the manual is to work for you, and can easily be achieved by entering new information as it is received, even if this involves the filing of a temporary handwritten note, which may subsequently need to be typed. This makes it a particularly appropriate candidate for word processing or computer treatment, which will ensure quick and easy updating.

The manual, along with all other administrative files, should be clearly labelled with its title in large letters on the spine for easy identification. You will want to have this particular item to hand as it will be in regular use, especially during the early development of the service.

Certain basic items of stationery will be required right from the start. Items in general use throughout the organisation will be appropriate for certain procedures, others may be adapted for library use, but some will need to be specifically designed according to the library's requirements. These may be designed and produced in-house, printed externally, or purchased ready-made from library suppliers. Examples of circulation slips, loan cards, etc. may have been obtained during visits to other libraries, with comments on their usefulness. These should be considered carefully, along with those shown in library suppliers' catalogues, for their suitability to your particular service.

It is also worth looking around at some of the retail stationery shops that carry stocks of attractive coloured labels and other matching items, e.g. drawers for card indexes, which may contribute to producing a bright and lively atmosphere in the library, and provide a means of buying small quantities of these items as required. The use of different coloured labels can also be tied in with a keyword system of stock arrangement and helps provide instant recognition of subject areas. This will give continuity and link the book stock with the subject files if the same colour coding and keywords are used throughout.

The design of all stationery is important, not just for aesthetic reasons but for a much more practical requirement, that of performing a function within the procedure itself. Each piece of stationery can contribute to the efficiency of that procedure. Certain records need to be kept in a particular format as part of the overall organisational records system, e.g. for accounting and auditing purposes. However, those which are being designed specifically for library purposes need to be simple but to fulfil a function other than that of merely acting as a written note of an action. For example, an order card or copy order form can serve as an accessions record, a cataloguing slip or even a temporary catalogue card. Book loan cards or forms can also be multi-purpose, as described in Chapter 8.

This is the stage at which the procedures are not only being set up, but are actually being put into immediate use. You are now ordering and receiving stock; cataloguing, classifying and physically arranging material. The information service, however limited, is now operational. It is time to contact the users again and inform them of some of the new procedures.

Circulate a memorandum outlining what is now available, emphasising that additional material and information can be obtained by the librarian from other libraries. Describe briefly how the material is arranged, and how it can be borrowed. Invite people to visit the library and find out more about what is there and how it works. Prepare a short introductory talk and conducted tour, however small the library may be. Demonstrate an online search. Once people can envisage the service, having physically been around the library, they are much more likely to remember it and to use it, particularly if it is attractive and well-signposted.

Draw up a plan of the layout and display it with a notice reminding users of the loan system. All notices and labels should look professional, and present information in a clear and unambiguous way. The basic rule to be observed when preparing material which combines instruction with publicity is clarity, brevity and attractiveness. If it is not possible to get professional-looking notices prepared, invest in some instant lettering such as Letraset, which is easy to use and can look particularly attractive on a coloured background, toning with the general use of colour in the library.

As with all the other procedures and records being set up, notices and labels must also work for you and promote a professional and efficient image of the information service.

7 • *Stock: selection, sources and effective use*

Selection

By now any donations promised should have been received, as well as indications from departments and individuals as to their particular information requirements. These will have influenced the core list of essential reference material and journals which you have already drawn up, as discussed in Chapter 3. This list represents the initial stage of selection, the two main criteria to be satisfied being (a) that the collection provides a nucleus of relevant material which will enable the service to get off to an early start, and (b) that it is a collection of maximum usefulness, i.e. items which will either provide instant answers to a wide range of anticipated regular enquiries, or the means of identifying other organisations that can act as alternative direct sources of information.

The main emphasis of this initial collection will be on material of a general nature, e.g. basic reference books and general journals, with a smaller proportion of specialist titles relating to the organisation's particular interests. More specialist material will be added as the service develops.

The number of copies of journals required will relate to what is already received by individuals and what is required for circulation. This should already have been indicated in the information needs analysis, but in cases where a full analysis has not been carried out it is worth circulating the core list of journals and asking individuals to indicate which titles they already receive and whether they wish to continue to receive these personally or to have their names added to the library circulation lists. This can result in a saving on the number of copies purchased. There should also be a space on this list for suggested additional titles.

In addition to this basic collection some items of loan stock may also have been suggested in the information needs analysis or otherwise requested. Loan stock should be built up gradually and at this stage only purchased in response to direct

---

CIRCULATION OF JOURNALS
_____

Name: Department:

Please tick where appropriate and return to the Librarian, adding any
other titles which you think would be useful.

Title	Already received	Retain/ Cancel individual copy	Add my name to circulation list
↑ Core list of journals in alphabetical order ↓			

Initial circulation note

requests or as enquiries indicate the need. It is therefore particularly helpful if books can be obtained on approval, giving the enquirer and the librarian the opportunity to assess their usefulness.

Selection of stock in business and professional libraries does not usually involve formal selection committees as it may in some publicly funded institutions. Stock is more likely to be selected through a combination of suggestions and requests made by both the librarian and the library users. Where there is already an established library which is being developed in new directions, selection starts with the revision of the existing stock, e.g. checking for the latest editions of titles which are still relevant to the new service.

Apart from the two main criteria already noted for the initial core collection, guidelines on other criteria to be fulfilled will have been indicated in the information needs analysis, e.g. how up-to-date the material should be; which subject areas should receive priority when selecting material. Price will also be a consideration, although sometimes, particularly in the case of setting up a new service, the criterion to be met is simply: how much does the organisation need the information? Some items or services, although expensive, may be the only available sources for certain information. If they are essential to the organisation's business, then it may be a case of not being able to do without that particular item.

The need for certain types of information to be immediately available may dictate the format in which it is purchased, e.g. if it is vital to have up-to-date share prices on a regular basis, the *Stock Exchange Daily Official List* would provide these in hard copy or microfiche form. A simple microfiche reader is not expensive and the cost should be balanced against the considerable saving in space – important in the initial setting-up stage. Such information is also available online via Datastream or the Stock Exchange's own databases. You will have to assess which is most appropriate in terms of cost and content.

Format is an important consideration when selecting stock for a new service. The emphasis in a business library is usually on current information, which will result in less book stock and more interest in newspaper and journal articles, cuttings files, collections of company reports, trade literature, industry surveys, statistical material, market research reports, card services such as Extel, loose-leaf publications, indexes and abstracts, and online services. Loose-leaf services are particularly valuable where there is a need for regular updating, as in the fields of law and tax. Examples are given in the core list, but other loose-leaf services are available in various specialist fields. A need for newsletters and bulletins on latest developments in the business field may also be revealed. Extra copies of newspapers may be needed, not only for circulation but also for cutting purposes. It is less expensive to buy an extra copy of a newspaper than to photocopy a number of articles each day, or make full-text printouts online.

How to find out what is available

You will already have had some valuable suggestions for stock from the librarians of other organisations. To find out about new items it is necessary to look at a variety of sources. First scan the daily newspapers as well as the specialist journals. You are not only looking for book reviews, but also for other items of interest which may be mentioned in articles on various topics, e.g. studies and surveys which have been carried out, leaflets and charts which may be available.

Publicity material on new books, journals and information services will appear with great rapidity and in sometimes alarming quantities as soon as your name gets on a publisher's mailing list. Such material will be in the form of catalogues and leaflets, sometimes with sample pages showing, for example, the sort of details given in a directory, or the page layout of a particular item. It is worth looking at as soon as it arrives as it often gives details of pre-publication discounts, which can be considerable but will only be available for a short period of time. Approval facilities may also be offered.

Publishers' complete catalogues can serve a number of purposes. They can give a picture of the subject specialisms of each publisher, which is quite important as in the business and professional fields certain publishers are recognised as authoritative producers of particular types of materials, e.g. Butterworth and Sweet and Maxwell produce a wide range of legal material, as do Tolley, who are particularly well-known in the field of tax publications. These catalogues can also act as a valuable resource for tracing items, particularly in a new library where other bibliographical sources may not be available.

Publishers' catalogues also list prices; type of edition, e.g. hardback, paperback, fiche; date of edition; number of pages; and inclusion of illustrations. They can usefully be filed in alphabetical order of publisher, and kept in a filing cabinet or box files. Leaflets on individual titles can be circulated to those interested in a particular subject area, as part of the selection process. Publishers are listed in *Publishers in the United Kingdom and their addresses*, as well as in the first group of major bibliographical sources which follows on the next page. *5001 hard-to-find publishers and their addresses* will help particularly in tracing 'grey literature'.

Most professional institutions and associations have a publishing arm and will send out advance notice of new publications to all members, in which case you will find a number of copies of the same leaflet appearing on your desk through the internal mail, as well as directly from the institution! The professional associations are usually the source of official standards and guidelines for the professions, as well as producing other publications. Universities, polytechnics and other educational centres publish working papers and research reports which may be relevant to your organisation's business. These may appear in summary form as journal or newspaper articles, or be mentioned in the various library and information journals and newsletters that are published, e.g. *Aslib Information; Library and Information News*.

Various stockbrokers and business consultants produce surveys on companies and industrial sectors. These are often quoted in the daily press, but it may be worth writing to some of the major firms to ask for details of their publications, some of which may be available free of charge. Their names and addresses can be found in Crawford's *Directory of City Connections*. There is also an ICC database of stockbroker research, whilst market research can be accessed on MAID (see Appendix 1). Company reports provide another valuable source of information, usually free of charge from the company secretary or registrar. Other useful material, again often available at no cost, is produced by the banks. In addition to their own journals, they publish economic reports on different countries, and guides on various aspects of setting up and running a business. A letter or a telephone call to the bank's head office will usually be all that is needed to get your name on the mailing list. Accounting firms publish a range of material, from client brochures to detailed texts. Although aimed at clients, they are usually readily available to anyone who expresses an interest. A number of publishers now put out a whole range of controlled circulation journals, available free to anyone who meets the criteria in terms of job title and type of organisation. Some of these are listed in *Benn's Media Directory*.

Although most government publications have to be purchased, a number of economic and statistical reports and summaries, e.g. *Economic progress report* (monthly) and *United Kingdom in figures* (annually, in pocket folder form) are available free of charge direct from the Central Statistical Office, which also publishes annually, in booklet form, *Government statistics – a brief guide to sources*. This lists the main government statistical publications, and the names and addresses of departments to contact for further help, and gives hints on how businesses can make the best use of government statistics. Again there is no charge for the booklet.

Finding out about publications and information services not only occurs when setting up – it is an ongoing task. Tracing material involves the use of a number of bibliographical sources, of which some are quite expensive, and others may be consulted only occasionally. Whether you choose to buy any of them depends on their potential usefulness to you, and the size of your budget. It is better to wait before committing yourself to purchase; see how frequently you need to trace what sort of material. Consult sources in a nearby public library – some are happy to handle such enquiries by telephone. The libraries of professional bodies will carry out searches for members. Your informal contacts can also be very helpful.

Apart from items already mentioned, such as publishers' catalogues and other lists, the main bibliographical sources to note, details of which are given in the core list, can be broadly grouped as follows:

(1) To trace books by author or title, use
   Whitaker's Books in Print (formerly *British Books in Print*)
   Books in Print (covers US publications, and produces a separate volume by subject)
   Whitaker's Book List
   British National Bibliography (also arranges by subject)
(2) To trace reference books specifically, look at
   Walford's Guide to Reference Material
   Top 3000 Directories and Annuals
(3) To trace government publications and technical and scientific standards, use
   HMSO Lists (available daily, weekly, monthly and annually)
   Departmental Lists (for certain publications available direct from the departments)
   Guide to Official Statistics
   British Standards Yearbook
   ISO Catalogue, for international standards (to trace foreign standards first consult the British Standards Institution. See Appendix 1)
(4) To trace journals by title or subject, consult
   Willings Press Guide
   Dawson's Little Red Book
   Benn's Media Directory
   Ulrich's International Periodicals Directory
(5) To trace newspaper and journal articles, use
   Research Index (available fortnightly; indexes the daily and weekly press by industrial and commercial sector)
   British Humanities Index (monthly)

Current Technology index (contains no abstracts) and various abstracting services in specific subject areas, e.g.:
  Anbar Management Abstracts
  PIRA Management and Marketing Abstracts
  LISA (Library and Information Science Abstracts)

Most of the above are available online, or in CD-ROM or microfiche form, as well as in hard copy. Databases may include full-text as well as abstracts. Select the ones most appropriate to your need by following the checklists in Chapter 5.

How to make the most of your stock

With such a diversity of format, apart from its organisation and physical arrangement, how can you ensure that maximum benefit is derived from the stock? Library users must be kept up-to-date with new additions. Not by the circulation of long recent additions lists on an occasional basis, but by notes to individuals when there is something which you know to be of particular interest to them; or by including new items or services with a brief description of their scope in any bulletin or newsletter which you may produce regularly. A bulletin giving summaries of the coverage and usefulness of six to eight current items will be much more helpful to the user than a list of authors, titles and classification numbers.

Scanning journals and newspapers takes time but is well worthwhile in that it keeps the librarian in touch with developments in the field, as well as providing material for subject files, indexing, abstracting, and inclusion in publications. In a specialist library the first point is particularly important, especially for those working without assistance, where the organisation relies on one person to provide a comprehensive and dynamic information service related to all its business functions.

The circulation of journals can be helpful to the librarian, as well as the reader. Specialist staff are often willing to scan in their own field and provide feedback on articles of interest for indexing or filing, as well as suggestions for purchase. The librarian can keep them aware of items noted in the general press. An alternative to circulating journals is to circulate copies of their contents pages, although this is not always very satisfactory in view of the great variation in the amount of detail given.

Once you have started scanning and noting items of relevance you will get much more of a feel for what the organisation needs and how its interests relate to the business environment generally. This could be the point at which to test out the usefulness of an information bulletin or newsletter, depending on the demands on your time and any assistance which you may have. The scanning is already being done, so items for inclusion in a newsletter will emerge from this. The only additional time required is for the writing of appropriate abstracts and the actual production of the newsletter. Criteria for inclusion will vary according to the organisation, as will the regularity of production. Each edition can be achieved in one to two hours of writing, if it is kept to two typed sides of A4 paper; plus the time for typing, printing and distribution. It can be weekly, fortnightly or monthly, although obviously the more current the material the better. Typical items would point out new developments relevant to the organisation's business. The user's interest can be aroused by the use of a short title which nevertheless reveals the topic under discussion, followed by a two- or three-line abstract of the main points and a source reference where appropriate. The items could be based on articles, surveys, and reports, or may give details of conferences and exhibitions noted from publicity material. They could also describe new publications or services, highlighting any aspects of particular interest, and can include news of other library developments.

Alternatives to writing a newsletter can be to circulate photocopies of articles individually, which can be time-consuming and expensive, and may not be welcomed by the user; or, as is done in some libraries, to be more selective and fit together press cuttings so that they can be photocopied in reduced form, with several cuttings appearing on one sheet of A4 paper. This may be more appropriate to some subject areas than to others. Another way is to print out the headlines each day from an online database and circulate or display them.

The newsletter, however, is popular with users as it summarises the material for them but allows them to refer to the full text if necessary; it keeps them up-to-date, and will not take too long to read if kept to two sides of paper. New members of staff may find that it provides a useful way of becoming familiar with the organisation's interests, as well as with the business environment; and associated offices who do not have a library can find it to be a valuable source of information. It acts as a means of two-way communication between the librarian and the users, in that the response enables the librarian to gauge which subjects and developments are of most interest, and to develop the service accordingly.

A practical way of organising for anticipated response to the newsletter is to number each issue and each item sequentially, and to keep a master copy of the original source material of each item in number order in a box file. Users can then request further information merely by quoting a number, and photocopies can be made from the master. This can work well on a self-service basis once users know how the system operates.

If such a newsletter proves successful and is to continue to be produced, it is a good idea to print it on paper of a distinctive colour, perhaps with a pre-printed heading, so that it is easily identified. A wordprocessor used for producing the master offers ease of editing and correction, as well as giving good layout with justified margins, and a professionally printed appearance. All or some of the abstracts included in the newsletter could be classified, indexed or incorporated into subject files or databases, if they are thought to have some future relevance. Scanning for newsletters and bulletins, and their role in the future development of the service, are discussed further in Chapters 11 and 12.

Displays of stock are well-established as a means of drawing attention to material, but they must look good. They do not require a lot of space, it is the style of the display that catches the eye. Use stands if they are available; but a small table, the top of a bookcase, or one shelf can be equally effective. Stand books upright; choose items with contrasting dust-jackets; scatter pamphlets in groups between the books; add some bookmarks, often provided free by publishers or bookshops, and an attractive notice indicating whether the items are available for loan. Do not have a display in the same spot each time, or too regularly, otherwise the impression can be that it is the same old display!

A notice-board offers another means of promoting the stock. Again the use of colour, and items arranged in an attractive way, can highlight pieces of information. It can also be used as an efficient way of making available statistical tables or other items which are regularly requested, e.g. the Retail Price Index, the Bank Base Rate, the latest library bulletin, or a daily printout of any online service in use. To be effective a noticeboard needs not only to be attractive and up-to-date, but also to play an active role in the provision of information.

As has been discussed, setting up a library or information service does not just involve selecting stock, but also considering the further implications of the material that has been selected, and how it can be used to maximum benefit. However, stock cannot be considered without the related administrative procedures of acquisition and processing which will make them a working part of the new service. These procedures will be described next.

Further reading

NORKETT, P. *Guide to company information in Great Britain*. Harlow: Longman, 1986.
ROWLEY, J.E. *Abstracting and indexing* (2nd edition). London: Bingley, 1988.
SPILLER, DAVID. *Book selection* (4th edition). London: Bingley, 1986.

8 • *Stock: acquisition and processing*

Having found out what is available and selected particular items as being relevant, the next step is to order them and get them into stock as quickly as possible. To do this you need to (a) develop an ordering procedure which gives you the various records required, (b) have a processing system ready to deal with the items as they arrive, and (c) find an efficient book supplier.

There are a number of ways of organising orders and every library will modify the procedure to its own requirements. Within a large company all items may go through a central ordering department, in which case the documents will be those in use throughout the organisation, with a copy being retained for library records. If, as is much more usual, the library makes its own arrangements for ordering, then order forms, cards or slips can be used if the ordering procedure is not automated. As with all other procedures, particularly where the resources of time and staff are at a premium, this one should be kept simple but should fulfil the functions required of it.

The method you choose will also relate to the number of items that are likely to be ordered, not just in setting up the service, but on an ongoing basis. Some suppliers are happy to accept telephone orders without a written confirmation, others take electronically transmitted orders, e.g. online, fax or telex. The most basic method is to adapt the organisation's headed notepaper as a standard order form. Slightly differing versions can be devised for each book supplier and the forms duplicated in-house.

These will act as top copies to be sent to the supplier, with copies for record purposes being made as required. A number of items can be ordered on one form and the copies can be filed in date order and/or by supplier's name. You will need to note on the copy whether the book is for library stock and for whom it has been requested, or whether it is being purchased for an individual or departmental collection. This is for purposes of distribution when the item is received, and to enable it to be allocated to a particular budget for payment. This method is suitable where small numbers of items are being ordered, but it does not allow

P and Q Associates

The Library, P and Q Associates, 27 Printout Place, Liverpool.

Date

B K Sellers (Book Suppliers)
4-5 Looseleaf Lane
Newton-le-Willows
Merseyside

ORDER FORM

No of copies	Details of publication	Price
1	EASTAWAY, Nigel A. and BOOTH, Harry Practical share evaluation. London: Butterworths, 1983. ISBN 0-406-19014-3	£24.00

Signed:

Typical order form

easy checking as to whether a particular item is on order, and it does not facilitate the checking-off procedure when books are received, especially if the invoice does not accompany the book and there is no indication of order date.

This method can be used in conjunction with an order record card which can be multi-purpose; the only disadvantage being that of writing or typing the information twice, i.e. on the order form and on the card. Copies of the original order form may not be needed, unless a file by date or supplier is required in addition to the order card, which is best filed by author or title. The card will need to be printed on both sides to include all the information required to make it multi-purpose, and again can probably be produced in-house.

The size of the card is arbitrary. You may wish to standardise all cards bought for the library, e.g. for cataloguing and for administrative record puposes, in which case 6 × 4 inch cards would suit most procedures. This also means that all record boxes, drawers or cabinets would be interchangeable, adding flexibility to the overall system. As has already been mentioned, such basic items as these can be used to contribute to the general attractiveness of the library, if colour and design are kept in mind.

The information on the cards can be varied to suit individual needs, but that shown in the example can be used initially to record order details, then as a follow-up when an item has not been received, e.g. a photocopy of the card can be sent to the supplier, and to record progress reports. Its next function is to record receipt of the item and to provide details indicating distribution. It can

ORDER NO.	ORDER DATE	ACCESSION NO.
FORMAT	FOLLOW-UP DATE	CLASSIFICATION
AUTHOR		
TITLE		
PLACE	PUBLISHER	DATE
PAGES		PRICE
SOURCE	FOR	APPROVED

SUPPLIER	
TRADE/ RETAIL/ FREE/ EXCH/ REV	CHARGE
INVOICE NO.	INVOICE REC'D
SUPPLIED	
PROGRESS NOTES	

Typical order card (two sides)

The Library, P and Q Associates, 27 Printout Place, Liverpool.

B K Sellers (Book Suppliers)
4 - 5 Looseleaf Lane
Newton-le-Willows
Merseyside

AUTHOR   EASTAWAY, Nigel A. and BOOTH. Harry.

TITLE/ EDITION   Practical share evaluation

PUBLISHER   Butterworths

DATE/ PRICE   1983   £24.00

DATE ORDERED   DATE RECEIVED

REQUESTED BY   Sylvia P Webb

Typical order slip

then be used as part of the processing, classification and cataloguing procedures, and finally be filed as an administrative record when details of invoice, payment and budget allocation have been completed. The card can then be referred to when details are required for budgeting, planning and reporting purposes.

Another method is to design an order slip which will fit 3 or 4 times onto a sheet of plain A4 paper. To have four slips to a page is preferred, as these will still measure 6 × 4 inches and can be inter-filed with other records. Although this could also be two-sided, it may be preferable to include less detail than is shown on the card, and to design it so that it works in conjunction with other records, rather than acting as a single comprehensive record. However, it is still possible to set it out so that it performs several functions.

Instead of using headed notepaper for this, the name and address of your organisation will appear on each slip, so that when the slips are separated for despatch to book-suppliers, each acts as a separate order form. The name of the book-supplier may not appear on the slip as you could, for example, complete four slips on one sheet of paper, then send them to different suppliers, but something as simple as the initials or name of the supplier can easily be noted on your record copy. For ease of handling it is better if the sheets are kept whole when typing or writing out the orders, of which either carbon copies or photocopies should be taken. The sheets can then be cut up, or torn if perforated, into individual slips. Such slips can be prepared in pre-printed and pre-carboned form, which makes them even easier to use, but will be more expensive.

If the sheet has been printed on two sides, then the order slip can be as multi-purpose as the order card, but as the name and address of the organisation is to

ACCESSION NUMBER	AUTHOR	TITLE	PUBLISHER	PUBLICATION DATE	PRICE	SUPPLIER	DATE RECEIVED
1							
2							
3							
4							
5							
6							

Typical page from accessions register

be included, there will be less space for other details, at least on one side. The slip can just as usefully be one-sided, with details of invoices and payments treated separately. All invoices could be photocopied on receipt and filed by supplier and/or date. The date that it is passed for payment can be written on the copy invoice. This then provides a suitable record for reference should there be queries about non-payment, and avoids the possibility of error which could occur when transferring details of invoice numbers to order cards. It also acts as a source of budget information.

The slips themselves can be filed by author or title and used for checking and processing procedures in the same way as the order card, although being on paper they do not handle or wear as well. However, the latter point may not be a consideration if they are only to be kept for a short period and are just for internal use.

After receipt of items, the cards and slips can be filed in an 'orders received' section until they have been processed and entered in the catalogue. This leaves items still on order in one small section and makes checking and follow-up much easier. Where formal cataloguing and classification are not carried out for any reason, the 'orders received' section acts as a basic list of stock purchased over a certain period of time, although this will of course be very limited in its usefulness in that items can only be checked by whatever filing order has been used, and it does not offer the opportunity for any other approach. As a temporary measure, however, it provides some means of checking stock.

The slips and cards in the 'orders received' section can be used in the processes of registering, cataloguing and classifying. In the case of books and pamphlets, registering involves noting on the copy order that the item has been received, marking it with a stamp of ownership, and allocating an accession number. This is the next number in a series and does not usually relate to the classification. Accessions registers involve entering each item received in order of its arrival, which determines its number, with details of supplier, publisher, date of publication and price. The details can be kept in written or typed form on punched pages so that they can easily be extracted or refiled in a manually organised register, or they can be entered into a wordprocessor or computer file.

This is a particularly useful record for audit purposes, and the accession number can also be entered on the order card or copy invoice for instant identification. It establishes the identity of a particular copy where there is more than one in stock.

Some libraries do not use accession numbers at all; others combine them with the classification and shelf location codes; but in both cases, where there is more than one copy, this needs to be noted inside the book for identification purposes. To register journals and looseleaf services which arrive regularly, it is usual to enter each issue on a visible index, indicating the date of receipt, and stamp it with a mark of ownership, before circulation. The card for each subscription will also carry a note of the number of copies ordered, circulation details, and binding requirements, as well as providing a place to note invoice and payment details.

The processes described so far in this chapter have been manual ones, but, as Chapter 5 indicated, there are software packages designed to cope with these various administrative tasks.

The mark of ownership is usually put on by means of a stamp and inkpad, either along the edge of the pages, on the cover, or inside it, depending on the format. An alternative way is to use pre-printed labels, but these are not as permanent as the rubber-stamp method. This represents the first stage in the physical processing of an item for stock.

Before going any further with the processing, it is necessary to classify the item so that the classification code can be written on the outside. This can either be written directly onto the spine of the book or the dustjacket with an electric stylus, or, more usually, particularly in a smaller library, on a label which can then be fixed either to the spine if it is wide enough, or to the front cover. If the latter, the top left-hand side as the cover is facing you is preferred as this is nearest to the user when looking for the item on the shelf.

As well as the classification code, which may be in number or letter form, the first three letters of the author's surname are often added to the label for ease of filing and finding on the shelf. Make sure that all lettering is neat and big enough to be read easily on the shelf.

Where books have dustjackets, these can be covered with clear film to preserve the jacket and the label, and to add to the overall attractiveness of the stock. The film can be bought in continuous rolls in sleeve form, so that the jacket is slipped into the sleeve, and any surplus material folded to the inside to ensure a good fit and a tidy finish.

There is also a self-adhesive clear film (Vistafoil) which can be cut to size for covering paperbacks, pamphlets and other items which do not have a dustjacket. This comes in a continuous roll, with the film attached to a coated backing paper, similar to that used with self-adhesive labels. It is cut to size then the backing paper is peeled off and the film fixed to the book or pamphlet. It takes a little practice to achieve a crease-free finish, but an instruction leaflet suggesting the best method of application can be obtained from the supplier, Don Gresswell. If film covers are not being used it is a good idea to protect the label by using clear spray coating or label protector tape. Unlike ordinary clear sticky-tape this remains clean at the edges and does not attract dust. However, it needs to be firmly attached to ensure that the labels do not get detached from the books. An easy way of doing this is to rub the handle of a pair of scissors over the tape, especially the edges, once it has been attached, as this will bond it into the cover.

Depending on the loan system in use, which is discussed later, this is the stage at which to affix date labels and pockets inside the front covers of the book, with the date label on the right-hand side to make for easier stamping. A book card will also need to be prepared.

If you are not using the book card system, then this stage will be omitted.

All the stationery and tools required for processing are illustrated with the various sizes and colours available in library equipment suppliers' catalogues,

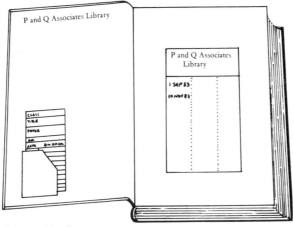

Prepared book

Don Gresswell's being particularly comprehensive and well set out. Processing will also at a later stage include repairing, so it is worth looking at the materials available, such as 'invisible' tape for repairing torn pages, reinforcing tape, etc. whilst leafing through the catalogues. It is important to use appropriate materials especially if items might need to be bound, or re-bound, at some point.

Library equipment suppliers are listed in Appendix 4. However, if all that you require are labels, felt-tip pens, stamp pads and a stamp, then your local office stationer is just as able to help. A good library equipment supplier is worth finding if you are going to be buying shelves, library furniture and larger items of equipment, as well as the stationery already mentioned. It is convenient to be able to order these from one source, as discussed in the chapter on physical planning.

The other suppliers with whom you will be making contact at this stage are the book suppliers. Even in the biggest companies, where there is a central ordering department, it has been found to be more efficient for the librarian to order independently. A central ordering department may have the responsibility for ordering electric plugs and nails for the maintenance department; coffee packs for the drinks machines; floor polishers for the cleaning section; and stationery and office furniture among other things. If the librarian orders independently there will be a number of advantages. The librarian can get to know which book suppliers or other information services are best to approach for which items. Some suppliers will be best for certain subject areas, others for speed of service, and yet others where items are required on approval.

One way of identifying the book suppliers most suited to your needs is to draw up a list of criteria and discuss these with other librarians who have similar requirements. You may have already received some recommendations on this during your visits to other libraries; it is certainly worth noting their experiences.

Your decision on whether to seek a sole, or almost sole, supplier will be based on the answers to these questions, and how many of the criteria can be fulfilled by one bookseller. If this seems to be possible it can prove to be a more efficient and time-saving way of acquiring stock, particularly where all items can be ordered on account, avoiding the need for cash-with-order payments. It may be necessary to have one main supplier, and several other accounts which are used less frequently, e.g. journal subscriptions and some standing orders for annuals and looseleaf services may be best placed direct with the publishers, particularly where pre-publication discounts or long-term (e.g. three–year) subscriptions may represent considerable savings.

A selective list of book suppliers is given in Appendix 3 but further specialist booksellers can be traced in the *Directory of specialist bookdealers in the UK* (details are given in the core list in Chapter 3).

Checklist 10: Book suppliers: typical questions to ask

(1) How wide a range of subjects is offered?
(2) Can foreign publications easily be supplied?
(3) Are government publications handled?
(4) Can publications produced by bodies other than commercial publishers be obtained?
(5) Do they handle periodical subscriptions?
(6) Is an approval service offered?
(7) Are standing orders accepted?
(8) Can all publications be ordered on account, and what sort of payment arrangements are available?
(9) Are there any handling charges, e.g. postage, delivery?
(10) Are there any discounts offered?
(11) How quickly are the items delivered and what arrangements exist for urgent orders?
(12) What means of delivery is used, e.g. by post, by van, etc?
(13) Are telephone, fax or online orders accepted?
(14) What is the preferred form for written orders, e.g. number of copy order forms?
(15) What details are given on the invoice, e.g: order date or number, author, title; does the invoice arrive with the order or separately? (This makes quite a difference to the ease of checking publications against orders, and to payment procedures)
(16) What other services are offered? E.g. what sort of items are held in stock; is there a retail outlet where purchases can be collected; do they undertake bibliographical searching or provide a cataloguing service?

Further reading

BOOTH, P. Selection and acquisition: books and periodicals. In: L.J. Anthony (ed.) *Handbook of special librarianship and information work* (5th edition). London: Aslib, 1982.

9 • *Classification and cataloguing*

The stock should be organised so that it is user friendly. It should be easy to find out if a particular item is in stock or whether a particular subject is covered, and equally easy to locate those items or subject areas in the library.

Some libraries with very small collections have decided not to carry out any formal classification or cataloguing, merely arranging books on shelves alphabetically by author or title, and putting other material in subject files. This has at least one major disadvantage: that of not covering for the eventuality of the item being temporarily removed. Without some form of listing it is impossible to tell whether an item is in stock or not. There is also no opportunity to search by subject – another important consideration.

Cataloguing

For the most effective use of the stock some form of cataloguing is vital. Most frequently the user will request an item by subject, author or title, so these would be the main headings required in a catalogue to enable the user to trace material.

A catalogue can consist of several sections:
- — a *classified* section – one where entries are filed in order of the classification scheme, usually referred to as the classified catalogue;
- — an *author* index – where all entries are filed alphabetically by the author's surname;
- — a *title* index – where all entries are filed alphabetically by title, discounting definite and indefinite articles, i.e. THE and A, e.g. THE PURCHASE BY A COMPANY OF ITS OWN SHARES would be filed under P;
- — a *subject* index – where subject headings only, not publication details, are filed alphabetically by subject, each card referring to the appropriate classification code under which that subject will be found.

Alternatively a dictionary catalogue can be used. This consists of all author, title and subject entries filed together in one alphabetical sequence, plus a classified sequence. For ease of use, a dictionary catalogue is favoured. The user does not have to look for the start and finish of several alphabetical sequences, and from the librarian's point of view it is much more flexible and easy to expand.

There are a number of different ways in which to physically organise catalogue entries, e.g. cards in some form of drawer system or cabinet, printed slips in looseleaf binders, a visible index, microfiche, lists stored on word processor or computer files. There are a number of software packages which are suitable for computerised cataloguing (see Burton and Petrie). Although automated catalogues are now in regular use in libraries of all sizes, card catalogues are also still widely used. Where the catalogue refers to a small collection, the card catalogue, particularly the single dictionary sequence, is still seen by many as being extremely user friendly in terms of speed and ease of use. This will be taken as the example throughout the chapter, which aims to describe the basic approach to, and requirements of, cataloguing and classification, rather than the theory and detail, already well covered in a number of texts which can be consulted at the Library Association and Aslib. It is the approach which is important, whatever format is chosen. The catalogue is set up to allow easy identification and maximum use to be made of the items listed in it. If you have not previously carried out any cataloguing or classification it is worth considering an initial discussion with an information consultant; attending a short course which includes an introduction to classification and cataloguing; and seeking the advice of other librarians working in libraries similar to your own. Cataloguing need not be carried out in-house; such services can be bought in via the British Library's BLAISE automated cataloguing services, or through various book-suppliers.

When setting up a library or information service you are in the fortunate position of being able to choose the method of cataloguing and classification most appropriate to the new service. You are able to draw on the experiences of other librarians. One such experience related to me was that of a librarian who took up a new appointment and found that there had been no cataloguing of material; classification of some items and not others; and very little labelling of stock. The shelf arrangement was a mystery known only to those who had been in the organisation long enough to know where the books they wanted were 'always kept'! If that is how it appeared to the librarian, think of the new, first-time user.

The user is the person for whom the service exists; the information must be organised so that it speaks for itself. Its arrangement must be self-evident, and the catalogue should work in the same way.

The amount of detail shown on the card varies from library to library, according to need. In most libraries the basic requirement will be to show the classification code, accession number, author's name, or names in the case of joint authors, the full title, the edition, series, publisher's name and date of publication. It is useful to show the number of pages to indicate the length of a work; and the price, should further copies need to be purchased. Although the price is subject to change, it can at least give an indication of approximate cost. It is also helpful to list any earlier editions in stock with their dates. If the work consists of conference proceedings, then it is appropriate to indicate that fact. Sometimes a cataloguing note will be required to highlight a special feature of which the user should be aware, e.g. useful appendices, format if non-book, but each library must decide on how much detail is necessary for its requirements, with its users always in mind. Each piece of information shown on the main card indicates a possible heading under which a further card could be filed, e.g. author, title, series. You will also need to select your subject headings for use in a dictionary arrangement or in a separate subject index.

There are a number of choices to be made about headings of all types, and if you are not already familiar with the cataloguing rules, then the *Anglo-American cataloguing rules* form the main point of reference. You will have to make such choices as whether to enter government departments under, for example, *DEPARTMENT* OF TRADE AND INDUSTRY, or *TRADE* AND INDUSTRY, DEPARTMENT OF, or even *INDUSTRY*, DEPARTMENT OF *see* TRADE AND INDUSTRY, DEPARTMENT OF; polytechnics may be called POLYTECHNIC OF CENTRAL LONDON or HATFIELD POLYTECHNIC – should you group them together? How do you cope with the publications of institutions, where the institution is far more likely to be known as the author, rather than the individual who wrote the publication? What about the subject headings for publications on more than one subject, or where there are several equally well-known terms for the same subject? *Sear's list of subject headings* is a useful source of reference for those sorts of decisions.

See and *see also* references are extremely helpful to the user in searching. A *see* reference refers to the preferred term, e.g. OVERHEAD COSTS *see* FIXED COSTS. A *see also* reference refers the user to other related areas which could be relevant, e.g. AUDIT SAMPLES *see also* STATISTICAL SAMPLING.

Tracings, i.e. notes on the back of the main card of all headings used for each publication, are invaluable to the librarian when withdrawing items from stock, or adding new editions, as they indicate all other cards on file for that item.

Whatever decisions you make on preferred headings, note them down and build up your own list of in-house cataloguing rules, along with a step-by-step list of the various stages of the cataloguing process, for the manual of procedures.

Another important aspect of cataloguing is the layout and presentation of the cards. The proximity of the heading to the top of the card determines the ease of use when looking through the catalogue. If the heading is too far down the card it will be difficult to see, particularly if the cards are fairly tightly packed in the drawer. It is a good idea to underline the heading under which each card is filed. This makes it clear to the user, and easier to refile if the card is removed from the drawer. All cards should be typed, and in the same typeface, with

CLASSIFICATION NO. (left margin)	344·106666 EAS
1 AUTHOR	EASTAWAY, Nigel A. <u>and</u> BOOTH, Harry.
2 TITLE/ EDITION	Practical share evaluation
3 PLACE/ PUBR/ DATE	London, Butterworths, 1983
4 COLLATION VOLS/ PAG./ ILL./ MAPS/ TABLES/ BIBL.	522 pp
5 (SERIES)	
6 ISBN/ PRICE	0-406-1904-3 £24.00
7 ACCESSION NO.	
8 NOTES	Very comprehensive index
ADDED ENTRIES/ HEADINGS	
9	Practical Share Evaluation
10	BOOTH, Harry. (joint author)
11	Share evaluation
12	

Cataloguing slip

consistency in the use of upper- and lower-case letters for particular pieces of information, e.g. authors' surnames and subject headings always in upper-case.

A cataloguing slip makes it easy for the typist to know how many cards are required and with what headings. If they are to be typed by someone outside the library, then example cards ensure continuity of layout. Use a different colour pen to indicate those items on the slip which will act as headings. The multi-purpose card or slip mentioned in the previous chapter could be adapted as a cataloguing slip or temporarily filed in the catalogue until the cards have been prepared.

Classification

The classification of material is another area where choices have to be made, the first being that of choosing a scheme most appropriate to the particular collection of information being put together. No classification scheme provides the perfect answer to the organisation of every collection of material. There are always sections which could be more appropriately grouped for your needs in a different way to that suggested by the scheme, even though the rest of it is suitable. It may be more practical in some cases, where a collection is small and very specialised, to use a simple key word system.

One such system which was set up and operated successfully worked as follows. The quick reference material was arranged alphabetically by title as that was how it was best known. The remainder of the book stock had a key word pencilled inside the cover of each item which was then filed alphabetically by that key word. In the case of more than one term being necessary to describe the subject coverage of the book, all terms were listed, the one used for filing being the first shown and underlined. For example:

GERMANY
ACCOUNTING STANDARDS
INFLATION

GERMANY was chosen as the main heading because the business interests of the organisation were international and the first approach was always by country. The catalogue contained cards under all three headings, plus a *see* reference: STANDARDS *see* ACCOUNTING STANDARDS, so that the book could easily be traced, whatever approach was used. The *see* reference was appropriate as the only standards used in that library were accounting standards and they were usually referred to as such. A visible index was used instead of a catalogue cabinet and proved very suitable for the size of the collection. The same key words were used for subject files which were filed in labelled boxes for ease of shelving. The books were not labelled due to low volume of turnover and actual movement of stock. For a larger, more mobile collection labelling would be required. The list of key words was stored on the word processor, making it easy to update and for a printed list to be made available if required. Key words were not used for the journals, which were filed alphabetically by title.

In-house classification schemes have been developed in a number of special libraries, but these do have to be thought out very carefully if they are seen as permanent ways of effectively organising stock. The alternative is to look at the various existing schemes with a view to using them either in full or more probably in part, e.g. the class covering taxation may be all that is required for a small tax library.

There has been considerable use over recent years of lettered classification schemes, particularly in business libraries. Letters are used instead of numbers, thereby providing a base of 26 symbols, i.e. A–Z, instead of 10, i.e. 0–9, on which classes can be built. One example of a lettered scheme is the London Classification of Business Studies (LCBS). This is a detailed classification originally drawn up for use in an academic environment where the subject interest was business studies.

Whilst some of the classes may not be appropriate for your requirements, this scheme does lend itself to easy modification. Each class can be lifted out and used on its own for a specialist collection. For example, Class E: FINANCE AND ACCOUNTING in conjunction with part of class P, i.e. PFCC-PFCX to cover taxation, could act as the basis for classifying an accounting library. Certain modifications would need to be made and certain parts expanded, e.g. PFCW – TAX ALLOWANCES is separate to all the different types of tax, e.g. INCOME TAX, CORPORATION TAX. In most tax libraries it would be more appropriate to have allowances with the type of tax to which the allowance applies. If the book is about allowances relating to a range of taxes then it would go under the more general heading for the type of tax, e.g. DIRECT TAXATION. Within Class E, the subjects ACCOUNTING and AUDITING are grouped together at EL. Whilst AUDITING STANDARDS has its own place at ELH, there is no provision for ACCOUNTING STANDARDS, other than that of using a form division, 739, from the auxiliary schedules, which are numeric. In order to avoid using both numbers and letters, and to cater for an important aspect of accounting, ACCOUNTING STANDARDS could be given a place within ELA – ACCOUNTING PROCEDURES, which could usefully be expanded. ELAB would be an appropriate place for ACCOUNTING STANDARDS. Two specialist schemes for accounting and business libraries have been developed in Australia; one by the Australian Society of Accountants for their own use and not publicly available, and the other by the Institute of Chartered Accountants in Australia, which is commercially available direct from the Institute.

Most libraries have a collection of quick-reference books, which are usually grouped together, separate from the main sequence, for ease of use, e.g. timetables, directories, dictionaries, street plans, hotel guides. Such items can be classified by subject, although some of them will be of a miscellaneous nature, e.g. *Whitaker's Almanack*. In a small library it is usually more useful to group these together by form. The auxiliary schedule previously mentioned, 700, will provide a list of headings but, again to avoid a dual notation, letters could be substituted for the numbers, e.g. this could become Class Z, a class at present not used in the LCBS.

In libraries where the interest is in more technical or scientific subjects, lettered schemes have been developed which have been kept simple in structure, and therefore easy to use, but at the same time give adequate cover to the subjects concerned. For example at the headquarters library of BP Chemicals a scheme was developed which combined the use of single letters with short number codes, e.g. within Class D – APPLICATIONS OF CHEMICALS, D1 = Adhesives, D2 = Construction materials; sufficient gaps were left initially to give the opportunity for future inclusion of new subjects within existing classes and also for additional classes, should they be required. Within each classification code, items are filed alphabetically by author. General reference material is put at the beginning of the scheme in Class A, scientific subjects follow in Classes B to H, with provision for non-specific subjects following in Classes J to L, which cover economics, management, marketing and other aspects of social sciences. It does not claim to conform to traditional classification theory, but no problems have been experienced in the use of the scheme by either the library staff or the library users. Although it organises material on a range of complex subjects, e.g. chemicals and chemical processes, it does not follow that the classification scheme itself has to be complex. The outstanding feature of the BP Chemicals Scheme is its simplicity. Such a scheme does require a comprehensive subject index. At BP Chemicals this is in the form of a card index, but could easily be developed using your computer or a word processor. The catalogue has a classified sequence, and a combined author/title alphabetical sequence, as well as the subject index. From a user viewpoint the single alphabetical sequence for author and title entries offers some of the advantages of a dictionary catalogue. Although the BP scheme was devised for a particular collection and may not be appropriate, as it stands, for other scientific libraries, it provides a working example of how an in-house scheme can be developed.

Beware the idea that mnemonics can easily be built into lettered classification schemes, e.g. Class M = Management. Developing a schedule then requires more the skills of a crossword designer than an information organiser! It offers no logical development, is open to misinterpretation and becomes an end rather than a means. If you require that sort of approach then the key word system previously described would be more appropriate.

As well as words and letters being used as codes to organise material, there are of course numeric schemes, the two main ones in use being the Dewey Decimal Classification (DDC) and the Universal Decimal Classification (UDC). Both are general schemes, i.e. when they were developed they aimed to cover the whole spectrum of knowledge, which was divided into ten main divisions. After this initial division the schemes differ in their methods of moving from the general to the specific, and in the degree of specificity available. UDC has the ability to show relationships between subjects by linking them with various symbols, e.g. brackets, colons, hyphens, and offers great precision of classification, but at the expense of simplicity. The very feature of being specific leads to cumbersome classification codes which are difficult to remember during the finding process, and whose sequence on the shelf, although in numerical order, is not necessarily easy for the user to follow. A number of special libraries do use UDC, and certainly both decimal schemes are worthy of study from the point of view of looking at the structure of a scheme, and the detail of its index.

Two other important general schemes which should be mentioned use a combination of letters and numbers, thus they are described as being alphanumeric. The first is that devised for the Library of Congress in Washington. The size of the library and its organisation into subject departments, suggests the possible use of one or more of the separate classes as individual schemes for specific subjects. Having said that it should be noted that most classes are at a different stage of amendment, therefore some will be rather out-of-date. The Bliss Bibliographic Scheme, also universal in coverage, has not yet been completed, but where a subject is well covered that class could again be worth considering for stand-alone use. A good example of this is Class J – Education. However, in a small library where the emphasis is on simplicity and ease of use, where more than a certain degree of detail is not required, then such schemes are probably not appropriate, or as with other schemes, would be best used in a modified form.

It is important that a classification scheme is up-to-date, i.e. that it allows for the inclusion of subjects previously not considered, because when the scheme was devised those subjects were unknown. A number of subjects in the fast-moving scientific and technological field will not fit appropriately into any existing class. Rather than putting a new subject into a class that is as near as the present scheme allows, revision of individual classes or the whole scheme may be necessary. Classification is a practical tool which must contribute to the overall organisation of stock and be an efficient device for information retrieval. If it does not fulfil both functions equally well, use another scheme.

When evaluating a classification scheme for use in setting up an information service, there are some basic questions to ask.

Checklist 11: Selecting a classification scheme

(1) Does it cover all the subject areas envisaged as being included in the new library over the next five years?
(2) Does it cater for general works as well as specialist subjects?
(3) Is it up-to-date and capable of expansion/modification?
(4) Is there a good index to the scheme, e.g. is it detailed, does it give cross-references to preferred and related terms?
(5) Is it easy to use, e.g. does it have a single notation, i.e. letters or numbers; can the codes be kept short; are the sequences logical and easy to follow?
(6) Could it be used in conjunction with a computer if necessary?

(7) Has it proved useful in libraries with similar needs?

(8) Which sections were found most appropriate in other libraries if the scheme was not used in full?

(9) Had any other scheme previously been in use in these libraries?

(10) What do they see as the main advantages and disadvantages of the present scheme?

(11) What modifications have been made by other libraries?

It is well worth discussing both cataloguing and classification with other librarians, before reaching a final decision on which system is best for the new service. Discovering the pitfalls of various systems, as well as their benefits, from those who have already tried and tested them, should help you towards a much more informed and appropriate choice for your particular requirements.

Further reading

Anglo-American Cataloguing Rules (1988 edition). Chicago & London: American Library Association and the Library Association, 1988.

Bliss Bibliographic Classification (2nd edition). London: Butterworth (continuous revision in progress).

BOOTH, P.F. and SOUTH, M.L. *Information filing and finding.* Buckden: ELM Publications, 1982. (Covers problems of indexing and classification, subject headings, construction of your own indexing scheme.)

BURTON, P.F. and PETRIE, J.H. *The librarian's guide to microcomputers for information management* (2nd edition). Wokingham: Van Nostrand Reinhold (UK) Ltd, 1986.

DEWEY, M. *Dewey Decimal Classification* (20th edition). Albany, New York: Forest Press, 1988. 3 vols. (Available through Don Gresswell Ltd in the UK.)

HUNTER, E.J. and BAKEWELL, K.G.B. *Cataloguing* (2nd edition). London: Clive Bingley, 1983. (Covers classification, indexing, filing, evaluation of retrieval systems, cataloguing rules, book indexing and the use of computers.)

INSTITUTE OF CHARTERED ACCOUNTANTS IN AUSTRALIA. *Classification schedule and relative index for accounting and business libraries.* Sydney: ICAA, 1987. (Available direct from the Institute at Box 3921, GPO, Sydney NSW 2000, Australia.)

Library of Congress Classification (4th edition). Washington: Library of Congress (ongoing publication in progress).

MOYS, E. *Moys classification scheme for law books* (2nd edition). London: Butterworth, 1982. (Currently out of print, but available from libraries.)

Sears List of Subject Headings (13th edition). New York: H.W. Wilson, 1986.

Universal Decimal Classification. BS 1000M. 1985. International Medium Edition. London: British Standards Institution, 1985.

VERNON, K.D.C. et al. (compilers). *London classification of business studies* (2nd edition). London: Aslib, 1979.

10 • Stock: loan and circulation

The choice of systems for lending and circulating stock will depend on the demand or need for such loan and circulation, i.e. in relation to the amount of material purchased separately for individuals and departments; whether the library is operated mainly by library staff on behalf of users or directly by the enquirers themselves; the number of library staff; and whether the library is to be used on a self-service basis. Other factors which contribute to the degree of borrowing by users will include, for example, the proximity of photocopying facilities; the convenience and attractiveness of the library as a place for consulting material, i.e. is there appropriate study space, does the user feel at ease; and the general publicity and promotion that the library carries out.

Loan

In a library which has been set up to play its part in furthering the firm's business, ease of access to information is most important. Restrictions and limitations on the number and type of items borrowed, and the period of time for which they are kept, may not be appropriate, particularly in a small organisation. As long as efficient records are kept so that stock can be instantly located and recalled as necessary, the loan system should be made as simple and flexible as possible.

The purpose of a loan record is to show where an item is, if it is not in its normal place in the library. The main systems in use in special libraries are still manual systems, involving the use of bookcards or loan slips. Automated loan systems are successful where there are large numbers of items issued. With the emphasis on information provision rather than the loan of material, this may not be appropriate to many special libraries. If you want to automate your loan system, see the further reading section at the end of Chapter 5. Some small libraries used to use a book in which to register loans. This is not recommended as it offers no means of locating particular items other than that of looking through every

CLASS:	
AUTHOR	
TITLE	
ACCESSION NO:	
DATE	BORROWER'S NAME

Single record book card

entry, and, unless used in conjunction with a date label, makes the checking off of returned items a very slow process.

The bookcard system may or may not involve the use of a borrower's ticket. In a small library it is more usual for the bookcard to be used to record details of borrower and date. This is much more convenient for the borrower and the librarian, involving the use of a single record, as well as less stationery and preparation time. It is especially useful in libraries operating on a self – service basis.

To prepare loan material for such a system, a book pocket to contain the card is glued into each book or pamphlet. Journals and other items may be treatd differently, although they are still seen as part of the loan stock. If a limited period of time is given for the loan, a date label will also need to be attached to the book or pamphlet.

Standard bookcards can be bought from library suppliers, or designed to specific requirements and printed. It is most economical to get them printed on both sides for maximum usage. The cards can be filed by date, author, classification code or borrower's name, whichever is felt to be most useful for the particular service. The placing of details on the card can be varied according to the filing order chosen, and it is worth showing the accession or copy number for instant identification. When items are returned it is good practice to cross through the borrower's name and date on the card so that, in the event of future borrowers forgetting to add their names, the previous borrower will not be bothered for a book which he or she has already returned.

Loan slips, either single- or multiple-copy, provide another simple means of recording loans. Although they require the borrower or the librarian to write more detail at the time of loan, this has to be balanced against the amount of time and stationery involved in processing each item of loan stock. Slips can be filed in the same sort of order as bookcards, i.e. by author, title, classification code, date or borrower's name. From the point of view of being able to locate a particular item, filing by author, title or classification code is preferred. If there is no time restriction on loans, then filing by date serves no purpose. The user may occasionally wish to check what is on loan to him or her, but unless large numbers of items are out on loan at any one time, it does not take long to go through the slips, so filing by borrower's name does not add to the effectiveness of the service.

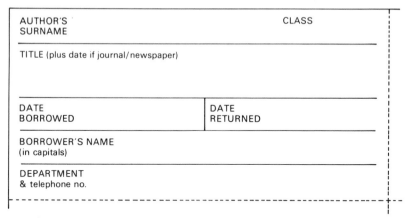

Loan slip

When the item is returned, the date of return can be noted on the slip, which can then be filed in a 'returned items' section. 'Returns' slips can be a useful source of reference for any analysis which may be required at a later stage. They can also indicate the need for additional copies or new editions which may appear in the future, or subject areas which could be developed. As long as they are well designed, slips can be used for all loan material, i.e. for recording the loan of journals, annual reports, subject files and other items as well as books and pamphlets. Single slips can be printed in pad form, with four or six slips to the

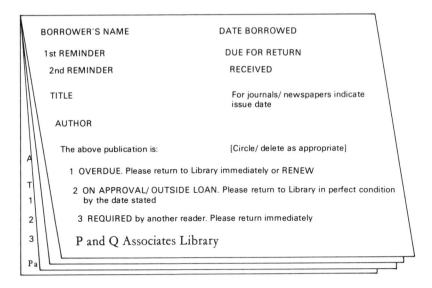

BORROWER'S NAME   DATE BORROWED

1st REMINDER   DUE FOR RETURN

2nd REMINDER   RECEIVED

TITLE   For journals/ newspapers indicate issue date

AUTHOR

The above publication is: [Circle/ delete as appropriate]

1 OVERDUE. Please return to Library immediately or RENEW

2 ON APPROVAL/ OUTSIDE LOAN. Please return to Library in perfect condition by the date stated

3 REQUIRED by another reader. Please return immediately

P and Q Associates Library

Multi-part loan slip

page for ease of use. The slips are divided by perforations. The borrower just completes the next slip and leaves it on the pad. The librarian then tears off each page as it is completed, separates the slips and files them under the appropriate heading. If the borrower has omitted any details, these can be added at this stage; it is also a good idea to underline the heading under which the slip is filed, e.g. author's surname, journal title.

Where there is a 'date due' system in operation, multiple pre‑carboned slips are useful.

After completion the top slip can be attached to the loan item, acting as a date label, and the other copies filed as the loan record in date order. A second copy, which will later become the return slip, can be filed by author or title in a separate sequence so that items can be easily located. When the item becomes overdue, a copy slip can be sent to the borrower asking for the return of the item or if renewal is required. Depending on the number of copy slips, a second reminder can be sent. Again, good design means that the slips can serve a number of purposes, including that of recording material borrowed from other libraries, or for potential purchase items obtained on approval. Multiple slips will probably need to be printed to particular requirements and are best produced in pad form with each slip in the set on different coloured paper, for example all top copies could be white, all first reminders green, second reminders yellow and 'return' slips blue. This aids recognition on the stage reached and further action required. In this case the pad is best made to the size of one slip, because of the carboning aspect and the fact that the slips tear off in sets.

YEAR & VOL.	JAN	FEB	MAR	APR	MAY	JUN	JUL	AUG	SEP	OCT	NOV	DEC	INDEX	BINDING DESP. RETD
REC.														
REC.														
REC.														
REC.														
REC.														
FREQUENCY			VOLS. PER YEAR			DATE NEW VOL. BEGINS			DATE COMMENCED					
TITLE						LOCATION								

Visible index: card to record receipt of journals

YEAR	VOL.	ISSUE	BORROWER'S NAME	DATE BORROWED	DATE RETURNED

Visible index: supplementary slip to record loan of journals

Where a single loan system does not cater for all types of loan items – e.g. the bookcard system is not appropriate for journals – then the single slip may be used as a secondary system to record the loan of all non-book items and items borrowed from other libraries. The visible index which records the receipt of journals can be purchased with supplementary slips which are suitable for recording journal loans.

In a case where there is very little book stock and the emphasis is on non-book material, or where the stock comprises a variety of formats, the single- or multiple-slip offers a more flexible loan system than the bookcard, but, whichever system is in use, it is important that the way in which it operates is clear to the user. This can be achieved by placing loan stationery in an obvious place with a brief but clear notice outlining the system. It is equally important to describe how to return items, i.e. where to put them, whether to check off the slip or card. If you expect users to put items on a 'returns' table or in a box, then label the table or box accordingly so that it is easily seen. Loans should be cleared as soon after return as possible so that the items can be refiled and made available for other users.

If your organisation is a member of various professional associations, you may find it convenient to borrow items from their libraries. You may also decide to use the British Library's interlibrary loan service, details of which can be obtained from the address listed in Appendix 1. In either case there will be a date limit set by the library making the loan. As many of these libraries are not obliged to make external loans, it is a matter of professional courtesy to ensure that such items are returned on time, or that renewal is requested in advance of the due date. To assist in this, make sure that the reader is aware that the book has been

---

P and Q Associates Library

EXTERNAL LOAN

This publication has been borrowed from another Library

PLEASE RETURN TO P and Q LIBRARY BY:

If you would like to renew the item, please let the Librarian know before this date

Signed: Sylvia P Webb

External loan slip

borrowed from another library. Design a slip which can be clipped on the front of the item, asking for its return to *your* library one or two days before it is due back in the library of origin. This will also help to avoid the situation of the borrower returning the item direct.

Circulation

Stock can be circulated for a number of reasons. Journals may be circulated regularly to individuals who want to keep themselves up-to-date in certain subject areas, and also make suggestions for any newsletter which is to be produced. Details of names for circulation can be kept on the visible index and

TITLE		ISSUE	
CIRCULATION	DATE PASSED ON*	SUGGESTIONS FOR NEWSLETTER	
↑			
— Names —			
↓			

RETURN TO P and Q LIBRARY

*If anyone is away, please insert 'Return' against their name and pass on without delay

Journal circulation slip

amended when necessary. If there are a large number of titles and/or copies, with different circulation lists, it is worth typing master sheets and duplicating enough slips in advance for ten weeks' circulation. Four slips would fit onto a sheet of A4 paper, which could be cut up and the slips filed in order of journal title, ready for use. These could be designed and stored on the word processor or computer, with the complete journals holdings and circulation lists. You may also wish to record the receipt of each issue in this way rather than use the visible index method.

Books on approval and specimen journals may also be circulated for comments on their suitability for stock. An approval slip can be drawn up if the multiple-slip system is not in use.

To . . . . Date . . . .

From: The Librarian

<u>ON APPROVAL</u>

The attached publication has been obtained

ON APPROVAL/ as a SPECIMEN COPY

Title   Price

Author   Date

Previous editions in stock

<u>ACTION</u> Please delete as appropriate and return both slip and publication to the Library

I WOULD/ WOULD NOT recommend this publication for
LIBRARY STOCK/ PERSONAL OFFICE COPY

Signed . . . .

Approval slip

To . . . . Date . . . .

From: The Librarian

STOCK REVIEW

Title   Date of Publn.

Author

<u>ACTION</u> Please delete or tick as appropriate and return both slip and publication to the Library

1) RENEW/ CANCEL Subscription
2) Obtain revised edition
3) Out of date but RETAIN
4) Other comments

Signed . . . .

Stock review form

Books which are already in stock may be circulated as part of a stock review with a stock review form.

Publications which are considered to be of immediate importance to your organisation should be taken into stock on arrival and circulated to appropriate individuals, with a brief note of your reasons for doing so, e.g. deadlines for comment to the issuing body, new legislation to be noted, mention of the organisation and/or its competitors.

There should be a section in the manual of procedures giving circulation details of types of publications, other than periodicals, which are produced regularly by various bodies, e.g. accounting standards, discussion papers, codes of practice. There should be a note of the ordering procedure, e.g. from whom, if by standing order, number of copies, as well as the names of individuals or departments to whom these are distributed.

There may be other types of material which it would be appropriate to circulate in your particular organisation; these may have been indicated in the information needs analysis. However much, or little, circulation is carried out, the key factor is speed, and all the forms and slips should indicate this to ensure that maximum benefit is gained from the material circulated. Both loan and circulation systems are set up to make it easy for the user to take fullest advantage of the information service. As with classification and cataloguing, these systems must be simple but effective. The information service in turn is then able to make a positive contribution to the business activities of the organisation.

Further reading

DOIDGE, R. Physical arrangement and display, circulation and loan. In: L.J. Anthony (ed.). *Handbook of special librarianship and information work* (5th edition). London: Aslib, 1982.

11 • Staff: development, qualities and skills

The quality and usefulness of a library service is not just a reflection of the material that is available or the way in which it is arranged. To the user the initial response to a request for information, the manner in which the information is sought, and the final presentation of the results are the criteria by which the service is measured. The staff represent the service, and act as the key to its potential.

To discuss the staffing of a library opens up a whole range of interrelated areas for consideration, ranging from organisational to personal details, e.g. recruitment and salaries, tasks and techniques, qualifications and experience, training and career development, personal qualities and attitudes. There are some excellent management books on recruitment, selection, interviewing techniques and time management, all of which apply to library staff as much as to any other group. Behavioural science theories of motivation and job satisfaction are equally relevant when considering the management of staff. These areas are important enough to merit separate study, and recommended reading is given at the end of the chapter. The theories themselves will not be discussed here; however, the relevance of their applications and manifestations will be apparent when considering the best use of staff resources, e.g. the division and balance of tasks will relate to job satisfaction, responses to enquiries will reflect attitudes, the setting up of efficient systems and techniques will result in the better use of time.

Whether operating as a one person library or with several members of staff, the role of the librarian is one that is based on relationships and continuous communication with individuals at all levels throughout the organisation. First, the need for an awareness of, and feeling of participation in, the structure and objectives of the organisation as a whole is essential. As recommended in Chapter 1, personal contact with members of the organisation should be made as early as. possible; the information needs analysis providing the initial mechanism for this. If additional library staff are appointed in the early stages they should also be closely involved in such communication processes.

Communication involves breaking down barriers, one of which may be that caused by 'the image' of a librarian in the user's mind. This may be an unapproachable, unhelpful character, surrounded by so many inflexible rules and regulations as to make the user feel excluded from, and an intruder upon, the library. Unfortunately, such stereotypes are not just a figment of the user's imagination, but they do seem to be a rare breed in business libraries, where a positive approach is essential. Along with all other departments, the library has to justify its existence by its contribution to the business activities of the organisation. The information for which you have just been asked may lead to making the next million!

What do you look for when selecting staff for a business or professional library? First, draw up a list of the tasks which need to be carried out, and the skills necessary to do so. These skills, which may relate to formal qualifications and/or work experience, must be matched with the personal qualities required for a 'good fit' into the department and the organisation as a whole. Qualifications may be in librarianship and information science or, if a subject specialist is sought, in other professional fields such as accountancy or law, or an academic discipline. Secretarial and keyboard skills are useful, not only for correspondence and the typing of catalogue cards, but also for any newsletters, bulletins or guides which may be produced. It is important that all library documentation has a co-ordinated style and professional finish. Work experience should be looked at carefully; the fact that an applicant has worked in industry or commerce can be more relevant than that of having worked in a library. There will be a familiarity with the business ethos, its objectives and terminology. Practical organisational skills are important, but like personal qualities these are not necessarily easy to spot at the interview stage, unless a personality test or work motivation inventory is carried out. The practical skills required are those needed for the efficient handling of the various tasks and procedures relating to the organisation and use of stock, as well as general administration. Personal qualities sought are those of helpfulness, enthusiasm, stability and flexibility.

Providing an information service in the business environment means working to deadlines. You and your staff are expected to be able to find whatever information is required, and to find it quickly. This requires the ability to be able to respond to pressure in a business-like manner *and* to remain pleasant and approachable in order to deal with the other enquiries that come along at the same time. The fact that you have a deadline is not the enquirers' problem, their main concern is the information that they want. So, in addition to a combination of patience and quick thinking, there is a need for the ability to organise work and to assign priorities to tasks. Enquiry work should always have priority over administrative tasks, and the enquiries themselves can be assigned a degree of urgency by making it routine to ask every enquirer how soon the information is required. It should also become second nature to establish exactly what the user wants to know, which may not be clear from the question first asked.

An efficient way of organising enquiry work is to design an enquiry form for all but the most basic enquiries, e.g. they would not be used for recording requests for addresses, timetable details, etc. The form would have the date and enquirer's name at the top followed by a space for the enquiry and the time by which the information is required. Sources tried, outcome and time taken are other headings to be given appropriate space on the form. In some organisations all work carried out for clients has to be noted with the time taken for accounting purposes. This can also be incorporated into the design of the form. The completed forms serve a number of purposes. First, they can be copied and passed to the enquirer as the response; they can be filed in date order as an administrative record; they can be referred to if a similar enquiry occurs; they can be analysed to establish the information requirements of departments and clients, as well as for planning purposes; they can indicate the most cost-effective ways of retrieving certain types of information, particularly where outside resources or pay-as-you-use facilities are used.

Knowing where to look and who to approach for information comes through training and experience. It can be a frightening moment when you are presented with a request for information, especially with a deadline on it, and you do not know where to start. Always start with your own resources, unless you are absolutely sure that they have nothing to offer. You need to get to know the full potential of your stock. Think of several possible approaches, e.g. different key words for a subject enquiry, alternative spellings or ways of listing a company name – could it be under the first part of the name even though it appears to be a forename; should there be a hyphen or not in the surname, in which case it may be filed under the first or second part of what appears to be a surname. Having exhausted the in-house possibilities, including specialist staff in other departments, try external sources, perhaps a colleague in a similar library, or the librarians of institutions of which your organisation has membership. Even if they have not got the information that you need, they may be able to suggest a likely source, such as one of those listed in Appendix 1.

There are a number of short courses, ranging in duration from one to three days, which can help develop your own or your staff's skills in enquiry work. Aslib runs a number of courses which cover the techniques of reference work and handling enquiries, as well as introductory courses at various levels for those just starting work in a special library. Courses are advertised in library and information journals and newsletters, as well as being listed in the 'Professional Calendar' – published six times a year by the College of Librarianship Wales. Outside the UK check with your professional associations and interest groups. The Aslib Economic and Business Information Group (AEBIG) organises various workshops and evening meetings on topics related to working in a business library, whilst TFPL and the Library Association run evening seminars as well as longer courses on various aspects of business information work. Schools of librarianship and information science also hold short courses which may be useful, and other groups listed in Appendix 1 run occasional conferences, hold meetings and arrange visits to various organisations which may have interesting libraries or run relevant information services. Membership of these groups will keep you and your staff in touch with developments in the field, and open up a number of avenues to external resources.

Another skill to be developed is that of scanning, in order to make maximum use of newspapers and journals. This is a skill which comes with practice and is as much a matter of knowing what to look for, i.e. what could be of interest to the organisation, as of quick reading techniques. To train staff who have not done any scanning before takes time, but is well worthwhile, in that they will be able to identify with the organisation more easily and give a better information service. They will also gain job satisfaction from having a task which is their responsibility. One way of organising this is for each member of the library staff to scan a particular group of journals, e.g. the economics journals. During the training period they will start by having an explanation of what subjects are looked for, why they are of interest, and what will be done with the information, e.g. abstracted for a newsletter, photocopied for a subject file, sent to an individual. As they scan, they should note the page number and indicate the particular article of interest where more than one article appears on a page. The supervisor of the training then scans the journal independently and carries out the same procedure and the results are compared and discussed. After 3-6 months, depending on the frequency of the periodicals scanned, supervision should no longer be necessary.

In a small library there should be a great deal of interaction between the staff, each member being constantly aware of what enquiries the others are handling and how they are carrying out various procedures. This provides opportunities for continuing learning and development from which all members of the library staff benefit, as does the information service. It maintains a feeling of involvement, increases staff confidence and ability, and ensures a consistent service. The smaller the library, the wider the range of tasks handled by each member of staff. The distribution of work should be balanced, so that each member of staff has one area which is his or her particular responsibility, and a range of other tasks which all the staff share. This is essential not only from the point of view of job satisfaction, but also to enable absences to be covered without any deterioration of the service. For the same reason, in a one-person library situation, where a member of staff from another department may be called in temporarily to cover for meetings and holidays, it is essential to try and organise a short overlap beforehand so that some sort of explanation of the service can be given. However basic this may be, backed up by a well-organised manual of procedures, it offers the temporary member of staff a certain degree of familiarity and a point of reference.

Where additional help is required, either on a regular part-time basis or on an occasional basis, there are several ways of solving the problem. A number of professional people want a part-time job because of other commitments, e.g.

other freelance work or domestic responsibilities. Such individuals can be extremely valuable in a small library with the expertise that they bring. If at a later date the need for a full-time member of staff becomes apparent the part-timer might increase the number of hours worked or another part-time professional could be added. The benefits of job-sharing have been described in a number of articles; they are certainly worth consideration. Occasional help may be available in-house; or, where there is a specific task of a certain duration, it can be worth employing temporary assistance. A student of librarianship or business studies could be offered this task as vacation work or as practical work which may form part of his or her course, in which case some training programme may need to be devised, or feedback given to the college. Alternatively, someone with appropriate skills could be recruited by advertising in the *Library Association Record Vacancies Supplement, Library and Information News*, and the daily press; or through an agency. Aslib Professional Recruitment Ltd provides a particularly helpful service, the fee involved being money well spent when balanced against the great saving in time that would be used up in dealing with application letters and initial screening. If you have short notice requirements, Aslib will try to find you someone within 24 hours. TFPL Ltd also provides a recruitment service, in addition to its courses and publications.

Figures which are often asked for when setting up a library relate to staff/user ratios and salaries. To suggest that the number of staff should be based on the number of potential users is misleading, to say the least. The library of any organisation has as potential users all members of that organisation. Some will use it more than others, some will use it personally, others via library staff; the type and complexity of enquiry will vary from library to library as will the number and variety of services offered. The buying-in of information and the use of online services all have an impact on the number and level of staff required. Such ratios have been produced and may be appropriate to certain types of libraries if used with full awareness of their limitations, but in the libraries for whom this book is written, the number of staff will relate to the range of services required, and the development and use of efficient techniques to provide them.

Salaries vary tremendously. They may depend on the scales already in operation within the organisation, and can relate to level of responsibility, sometimes measured in terms of staff numbers; qualifications; previous work experience and achievement; or present and ongoing performance. The Library Association publishes regularly revised guidelines on salaries in different types of libraries, which provide a valuable starting point when recruiting library staff, but will tend to be more useful in suggesting a minimum level which should generally be observed, rather than specific figures for each appointment, which would not be possible, given the complex variations of each situation. Incomes Data Services (see Appendix 1) produces some useful guides to general pay and conditions of service in Europe.

The recruitment and training of staff is part of the librarian's management function. Staff organisation is an ongoing process and there are two-way benefits; to the staff and to the information service. Appraisal interviews should give the individual the opportunity to appraise the organisation, as well as be appraised by his or her manager. Such interviews, if well carried out, can lead to positive developments and changes for both the individual and the organisation. Formal appraisal interviews usually take place every six or twelve months, but there should always be the opportunity for discussion. Tasks and techniques should be regularly reviewed to see if they can be more efficiently organised; all library staff should be encouraged to give their own views on possible new developments and suggest improvements to the service. It is a great motivator to attend a meeting or short course outside the organisation, where new contacts are made and problems are put into perspective. Make sure that all the staff have this opportunity, even if it can only be occasional. The benefit to them will be shown in the improvement in the service; they represent one of the most valuable resources.

Further reading

BEATTIE, D. *Company administration handbook* (6th edition). Aldershot: Gower, 1988. (Part 5 gives detailed coverage of employment practice and law.)

HIGHAM, Martin. *The ABC of interviewing.* London: The Institute of Personnel Management, 1979.

JANNER, G. *Meetings.* Aldershot: Gower, 1988. (Audio manual series).

Job sharing: an introductory guide. London: New Ways to Work, 1988 (pamphlets).

JONES, N. and JORDAN, P. *Staff management in library and information work.* Aldershot: Gower, 1987.

LAWSON, Ian. *Appraisal and appraisal interviewing.* London: Industrial Society, 1987.

MURRELL, H. *Motivation at work.* London: Methuen, 1976.

PLUMBLEY, P.R. *Recruitment and selection* (4th edition). London: Institute of Personnel Management, 1985.

PRYTHERCH, R. (ed), *Handbook of library training practice.* Aldershot: Gower, 1986. (Contains a chapter on publicity and promotion.)

SIMPSON, W. *Motivation.* London: Industrial Society, 1983.

SPECIAL LIBRARIES ASSOCIATION (USA). *Time management in the small library.* (Computer assisted study pack.) Washington: SLA, 1988.

TURNER, P. and HAWKINS, K. *Time management made easy.* London: Grafton Books, 1985.

WRIGHT, C. *Selection interviewing.* London: Industrial Society, 1988.

12 • *What next? – future developments*

The library has been set up and is now operational; systems and procedures have been developed and put into action; the enquiries are coming in – what next? The future is a combination of ongoing tasks; review and modification; and further initiatives and developments. Perhaps it has not been possible in the initial process to put into operation all the services or procedures previously described. Go back to the checklists and reconsider various aspects. For example, if you have been using your computer mainly for one task, consider some further applications. The day-to-day running of the service involves the whole range of tasks mentioned in the previous chapters. Management control systems could need reconsideration. Items of stock continue to be ordered; new material will need to be classified, catalogued, processed; enquiries will increase in number, they may be made in person, by telephone, or in writing. Communication networks and mechanisms will emerge, all-important for maintaining constant contact with the users, letting them know what is available, whilst keeping you aware of their information needs. The information service should be a dynamic focal point for the organisation, not only responding to expressed needs, but predicting requirements and taking initiatives, becoming fully integrated as a vital part of the organisation. In order to be of maximum usefulness any developments need to be publicised. Users also need to be constantly reminded of the whole range of information services that are available. Promotion and publicity is always required, and can be achieved by regularly producing and distributing newsletters, bulletins and information sheets of various kinds. Presentations are not just important in the setting up stage. There is a regular need to keep people aware of what can be provided and of the changing nature of the service. Client interviews and surveys can play a key role in this and provide valuable pointers for the future, based on the user's evaluation of the service. Examples of these are referred to on pp. 18–19 of *Personal development in information work*.

The feedback from these in terms of requests for further details or photocopies provides a very good indication of the ongoing interests and information requirements of individuals, as well as a means of personal contact. It is also likely to generate more use of the library, as it will create an awareness of how much information is in fact available. If you have not already started some sort of bulletin, now is the time to circulate a trial issue and test the response. If a newsletter is well thought out it can make an extremely useful contribution to the business activities of a company or firm, as well as providing a mechanism for regular liaison with all parts of the organisation. Linked to this will be other aspects of SDI (selective dissemination of information); that is the sending out of information, e.g. cuttings or articles, on topics of specific interest to particular individuals. Your increasing knowledge of the organisation and its members, based initially on the information needs analysis, and now on your personal experience, will indicate more clearly the future directions for such SDI. Again, technology could play a useful part in this, e.g. electronic mail.

Try to keep up with personnel movements and changes so that individuals changing departments continue to receive information, stock can be retrieved if someone leaves, and new staff are made aware of the usefulness of the library service. This last may be by means of an introductory talk on an individual basis, or presentations to groups of new staff. In both cases these need to be interesting and lively, describing what the service can do rather than putting too much emphasis on the classification scheme in use or loan procedures. These can be outlined in a brief practical written guide which is handed out as a back-up to the presentation. A library guide can consist of information in the form of text or diagrams presented as hard copy, in slide/tape format or as a computer presentation. As part of their printed *Guide to United Kingdom company information*, Warwick University Library has developed a guide to tracing company information in the form of a logical network, i.e. as a series of boxes linked by lines with arrows leading on to the next logical step. This design can be adapted in printed form to suit almost any specialist collection of material, and provides a very clear step-by-step approach to searching. Reinforcement of such presentations can be achieved by the use of labels and notices in the library itself. These should be attractive, clear and co-ordinated, acting together as a straightforward guide to the stock and its use.

Policies should be thought out for reviewing stock, binding journals, microfilming material, and developing databases. The procedures and records already set up should be reviewed and revised where necessary. Thought should be given to interlibrary loan: could it be used more or less, does its cost suggest more purchasing and less borrowing, does it provide a quick enough response to your users' requirements, are some libraries more useful than others as sources for loan in the light of experience? It could be worth drawing up a list of which sources are best to approach for each subject area or type of material.

As the previous discussion indicates, running an information service requires the use and development of speaking and writing skills. This could also lead to

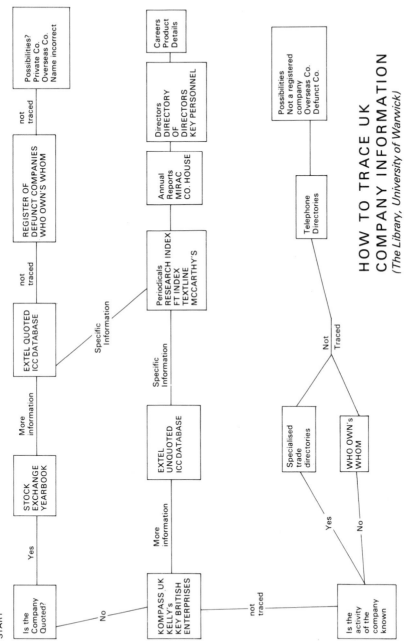

HOW TO TRACE UK
COMPANY INFORMATION
(The Library, University of Warwick)

involvement with publications produced by other sections of the organisation, perhaps in editing the material as well as researching the subject. Organising and distributing, as well as maintaining a collection of in-house publications, could be an additional responsibility and add a public relations function to the librarian's role.

Contact with, and use of, external information resources is likely to increase as time goes on, and is interlinked with decisions on the development of internal resources, e.g. the ease with which certain material can be located and consulted elsewhere will affect your purchasing decisions; the cost and availability of abstracting and indexing services such as those mentioned elsewhere will influence your thoughts on whether to carry out any in-house journal indexing. The full potential and possible limitations of your own stock will become apparent as each item is put to the test as a source of information. If you are receiving regular enquiries for information on companies, a subscription to the services of Extel could be useful. Extel offers a card service giving detailed financial information on both UK and foreign companies, and is updated daily. Their Exstat database gives similar information. ICC provides another excellent source of company and industry information through its databases and publications. Further details of these and the other services mentioned can be obtained from the addresses given in Appendix 1.

Now is the time to start looking at some more online services and the further use of computers and word processors in various library procedures. The Woodside example noted in Chapter 5 points to the broader role of the librarian in records management. The impact of technology on libraries has received a lot of coverage in professional journals, but one of the best ways of finding out what is offered is to look again at the services in action. Demonstrations of commercial databases, such as those available through Dialog or Datastar can be arranged free of charge, e.g. the database hosts may send a representative to your premises to make a presentation, or you might be invited to their centre for a demonstration and the opportunity to try out the databases yourself. Free trials of up to one month have been offered to certain types of libraries by both Textline and Datastream. You could also put a proposal to your organisation for a short project with a limited budget whereby you can test and evaluate a number of services in-house in a 'live' information situation, i.e. in the library as alternative means of answering enquiries. Consult other librarians about their experiences of various databases and their usefulness. Seek the further advice of online specialists, e.g. those at Aslib's Information Resources Centre, or contact the University of London's Central Information Services, who also organise some excellent practical courses in this areas. Now that you have a better idea of the emphasis of your service, look at as wide a range of services as possible to see which would be most relevant to your future requirements, e.g. if you regularly require references to press coverage of companies, industries and sectors, then Textline would be appropriate; but if you require business and economic information in statistical form, with the ability to manipulate data, Datastream or ICC may be the answer. A comprehensive evaluation of business databases, *Online business sourcebook* is particularly helpful and includes updating supplements to cover new services. Guides to specialist databases are published by Aslib; subjects covered include building, construction and architecture; business and companies; law; management and marketing; medicine; and patents and trademarks. It is also worth subscribing to *Online Review*, an excellent bi-monthly journal which provides a means of keeping up to date with what is happening in the field, backed up by comparisons and studies of the efficiency of various services, and practical advice on getting the best out of online, through training and efficient management.

Cost is an important factor when considering online, the main difference being between subscription services where an annual amount is paid for unlimited use, e.g. Textline; or a pay-as-you-use system such as Dialog operates. Datastream uses a slightly different method of charging, offering either an annual subscription to the complete service with unlimited use, or a nominal monthly subscription plus pay-as-you-use according to the programs selected. Given these variables you may decide not to subscribe to certain databases, but to buy in searches as required through an external service such as those offered by the London Business School or the British Library.

The question to ask of all information services, online or not, is do they provide the information required in an appropriate format, quickly, easily, and reliably, at an acceptable cost? The costs involved are not only those of buying a book or journal, or paying for the use of each database. There are costs in terms of staff time, training, equipment maintenance and enhancement, and the use of space. Equipment is being improved so rapidly, with an ever-increasing number of items on the market, that it is worth doing some careful research before upgrading. As a user of particular computer systems you will benefit enormously from joining one of the user groups. The Institute of Information Scientists will have details of these. These provide a valuable forum for discussion and you stand to learn a great deal from the other members.

Not all information is available online, and that which is should be seen as only part of the total range of information available. The need for other additional types of information will have been indicated by the types of enquiry already received. For example, regular requests for trade literature could make it worthwhile building up your own collection; enquiries in the area of marketing and advertising may suggest subscriptions to additional journals like *Campaign* or indexes such as *Marketing Surveys Index*, or *Reports Index*; or the use of specialist databases such as MAID (address in Appendix 1).

You may have become aware of the usefulness of particular organisations as sources of information; consider taking out individual or corporate membership where this is possible. If you have found that there is no librarians' group within your organisation's main interest area, but that there are in fact a number of such librarians, why not sound out the possibility of setting up a group? Where there are such interest groups, active participation by all members is essential if everyone is to benefit. Apart from regular, although not necessarily frequent meetings, members keep in touch by circulating new publications, contributing items of interest to any group newsletter produced, offering reciprocal arrangements in terms of loans or photocopies, and generally responding to each other's occasional calls for help in finding information. The meetings themselves provide a learning situation as well as a social occasion, with the opportunity to listen to outside speakers on their particular areas of expertise; to exchange news with colleagues and to learn of ways in which they have resolved certain issues or developed new ideas. There is the possibility of collaboration in a joint venture, e.g. designing a training programme tailormade to the needs of a specific type of library; or working on classification problems.

Staff development, including your own, is a vital ingredient of your planning for the future. Without skilled and motivated staff the service itself will not develop. This whole area is the subject of another book, *Personal development in information work*, which tells you how to identify the areas most appropriate for each individual, whilst not losing sight of the need to match these to those of the service. Courses and conferences which could help in this are listed in the bimonthly *Professional Calendar* published by the College of Librarianship Wales.

Participation in the activities of both formal and informal groups provides an invaluable means of keeping up-to-date with developments in your own area of interest, and with current activities in information work generally. This is an ever-changing field, with increasingly wider horizons. New sources of information and systems with which to organise them continue to appear.

At the beginning of this chapter a question was asked – 'What next?' The fact that the answer is always changing is no reason to stop asking the question. That way you will continue to develop and give a relevant and effective information service.

Further reading

Campaign. London: Marketing Publications. Weekly.
INSTITUTE OF CHARTERED ACCOUNTANTS IN ENGLAND AND WALES. *Management control: guidance to good practice statement*. London: ICAEW, 1986.
KINNELL, M. (ed.). Planned public relations for libraries. London: Taylor Graham, 1988.
Marketing Surveys Index. London: Marketing Surveys Index. Monthly. Also available online.
Marketsearch. International directory of published market research. London: Arlington Management Ltd. Annual, with updating service.
Outlook on Research Libraries: an international bulletin. Oxford, New York, Amsterdam: Elsevier Advanced Technology Publications. Monthly.
PARTRIDGE, W.G.McD. *Low budget librarianship: managing information in developing countries*. London: Library Association, 1988.

Professional Calendar. Forthcoming courses and conferences for the library and information professions. Aberystwyth: College of Librarianship Wales. Bimonthly.

Reports Index. Dorking: Business Surveys. Bimonthly. Also available online.

RITCHIE, Sheila (ed.). *Modern library practice* (2nd edition). Buckden: ELM Publications, 1982.

STOAKLEY, R. *Presenting the library service.* London: Clive Bingley, 1982.

TURPIE, G. (ed.). *UK online search services* (3rd edition). London: Aslib, 1988.

WEBB, S.P. *Personal development in information work.* London: Aslib, 1986.

WOOD, L. and HAIGH, R. (eds.). *The future of industrial information services.* London: Taylor Graham, 1988. (Contains several pages on planning.)

Appendix 1 • *Organisations to approach for information (including special interest groups)*

Some of the following services are intended for members only but librarians are usually very willing to help other librarians seeking information.

ORGANISATION	COVERAGE
Aslib, The Association for Information Management Information House 26-27, Boswell Street London WC1N 3JZ Tel: 01-430 2671	All aspects of the library and information profession.
BACIE **(British Association for Commercial and Industrial Education)** 16 Park Crescent London W1N 4AP Tel: 01-636 5351	All aspects of vocational education and training. Courses, publications.
Bank of England Reference Library Threadneedle Street London EC2R 8AH Tel: 01-601 4846	UK and overseas coverage in banking and financial economics.

BBC Data Enquiry Service
Room 7
1 Portland Place
London W1A 1AA
Tel: 01-927-5998

Political, social and economic events, wide-ranging biographical information, business interests, industrial information, world statistics and the arts. Available on subscription or for occasional use.

British Institute of Management Library
Management House
Cottingham Road
Corby
Northants
Tel: (0536) 204222

General management, examples of company practice, and management training.

British Library Business Information Service
Science Reference and Information
    Service
25 Southampton Buildings
Chancery Lane
London WC2A 1AW
Tel: 01-323 7454 – free brief
    enquiries
    01-323 7979 – charged
    services

Company information, industry, country and market surveys, manufacturers' catalogues, electoral registers, law, statistics, official publications.

British Standards Institution
Enquiry Section
Linford Wood
Milton Keynes MK14 6LE
Tel: (0908) 320033

All information relating to UK and foreign standards.

Central Statistical Office
Great George Street
London SW1P 3AQ
Tel: 01-270 6363

All official statistics, and useful free booklets and statistical information in handy pocket folders.

City Business Library
Gillett House
55 Basinghall Street
London EC2V 4BX
Tel: 01-638 8215/6

Current business and company information, market data, other business topics. An extremely comprehensive collection.

Companies House
55 City Road
London EC1Y 1BB
Tel: 01-253 9393

UK company annual accounts.

Companies Division (DTI)
10–18 Victoria Street
London SW1H 0NN
Tel: 01-215 7877

UK and EEC legislation; part of the Department of Trade and Industry.

Daily Telegraph Information Service
Peterborough Court
South Quay
181 Marsh Wall
London E14 9SR
Tel: 01-538 5000

General telephone enquiry service.

Data Protection Registrar's Office
Springfield House
Water Lane
Wilmslow
Cheshire SK9 5AX
Tel: (0625) 535777

Advice on, and administration of, all UK data protection legal requirements.

Datastream
Monmouth House
58-64 City Road
London EC1Y 2AL
Tel: 01-250 3000

Company, economic and market statistics (online service).

European Communities Commission Information Unit
8 Storey's Gate
London SW1P 3AT
Tel: 01-222 8122

Extel Statistical Services Ltd
37–45 Paul Street
London EC2A 4PB
Tel: 01-251 1437

Detailed UK and overseas company information in the form of a card service.

Guild Sound and Vision
6 Royce Road
Peterborough
PE1 5YB
Tel: (0733) 315315

A wide range of training films and other material.

House of Commons Library
Westminster
London SW1A 0AA
Tel: 01-219 4272

Parliamentary matters.

Incomes Data Services Ltd
193 St John Street
London EC1V 4LS
Tel: 01-250 3434

Wide range of regularly updated publications on all aspects of pay and conditions of work.

Industrial Marketing Research Association (IMRA)
11 Bird Street
Lichfield
Staffs. WS13 6PW
Tel: (0543) 263448

Industrial marketing, related standards and consultancy.

Industrial Society Information Service
Peter Runge House
3 Carlton House Terrace
London SW1Y 5DG
Tel: 01-839 4300

Wide range of management, personnel and industrial relations subjects.

Institute of Information Scientists
44 Museum Street
London WC1A 1LY
Tel: 01-831 8003

Will help with enquiries on professional recruitment, qualifications, remuneration. Has a number of active interest groups and publications.

Institute of Personnel Management
IPM House
Camp Road
London SW19 4UW
Tel: 01-946 9100

Personnel management, industrial relations and employment law.

International Chamber of Commerce
Centrepoint
103 New Oxford Street
London WC1A 1QB
Tel: 01-240 5558

International trade; also produces publications.

Library Association
7 Ridgmount Street
London WC1E 7AE
Tel: 01-636 1544

All aspects of the library and information profession, publications, continuing education.

Library Equipment Centre
College of Librarianship Wales
Llanbadarn Fawr
Aberystwyth SY23 3AS
Dyfed, Wales
Tel: (0970) 3181

See Chapter 4.

Library and Information Technology Centre
Polytechnic of Central London
235 High Holborn
London WC1V 7DN
Tel: 01-430 1561

General enquiry service, demonstrations of library and information systems, publications, consultancy.

London Business School Library
Sussex Place
Regent's Park
London NW1 4JA
Tel: 01-262 5050

All aspects of business studies and related subjects. Also offers a separate commercial information service.

London Chamber of Commerce and Industry
69 Cannon Street
London EC4N 5AB
Tel: 01-248 4444

Company information files, a large reference section, customs and excise regulations.

London School of Economics Library
Houghton Street
London WC2A 2AE
Tel: 01-405 7686

Economics, politics, sociology, law, history, UN and US Federal documents.

M.A.I.D. Systems Ltd
Maid House
26 Baker Street
London W1M 1DF
Tel: 01-935 6460

Online database giving full text international market research reports and market activities.

New Ways to Work
309 Upper Street
London N1 2TY
Tel: 01-226 4026

Special interest in job-sharing, produces publications.

Royal Institute of British Architects Office Library Service
RIBA Services Ltd
66 Portland Place
London W1N 4AD
Tel: 01-251 5885

See Chapter 4.

Small Firms Centre
Ebury Bridge House
2 Ebury Bridge Road
London SW1W 8QD
Tel: 01-213 5133

Produces a number of useful booklets and offers consultancy.

Special Libraries Association
1700 18th Street NW
Washington DC
20009
USA
Tel: 010 (1) 202 234 4700

All matters relating to special libraries. Runs courses and conferences. Produces quarterly journal.

Statistics and Market Intelligence Library (SMIL), and Product Data Store (PDS)
1 Victoria Street
1 London SW1H 0ET
SMIL Tel: 01-215 5444/5445
PDS Tel: 01-215 4376

SMIL and PDS is a combined service provided by the Department of Trade and Industry to give access for UK exporters to a wide collection of detailed overseas official statistics, trade directories, development plans and other published information on overseas (i.e. non-UK) markets. PDS is a computerised microfilm database of product and industry-based information about overseas markets.

Textline
Reuter Textline
68 – 74 Carter Lane
London EC4V 5EA
Tel: 01-248 9828

Online service giving UK and overseas press coverage on companies and sectors.

Work Research Unit Library
ACAS
Room 111
27 Wilton Street
London SW1X 7AZ
Tel: 01-210 3895

Advice and information on the work environment, job satisfaction and related areas.

For the libraries of UK professional and trade associations consult the *Directory of British associations*; for government department libraries check the *Guide to government department and other libraries*. Details of both these publications are given in the Core List at the end of Chapter 3, as are details of non-UK directories giving similar information. There will also be locally published directories specific to each country.

SPECIAL INTEREST GROUPS

For details of the numerous branches and groups of the professional associations, contact the individual associations. The Library Association produces an excellent printed guide to its groups. Listed below are details of some independent groups. Others can be traced by checking with those already working in organisations in your specific area of interest.

Accountancy Library and Information Group
Contact: Mrs Pat Thomson
          Librarian
          Arthur Andersen & Co.
          1 Surrey Street
          London WC2R 2PS   Tel: 01-836 1200

**Association of Information Officers in
the Pharmaceutical Industry (AIOPI)**
Contact: Janet Taylor
          Leclerle Laboratories
          Cynamid of Great Britain Ltd
          Fareham Road
          Gosport
          Hants. PO13 0AS   Tel: (0329) 224000

Association of UK Media Librarians
Contact: Sarah Adair
       Kent House
       Upper Ground
       London SE1 9LT   Tel: 01-261 3734

Bank Librarians' Group
Contact: The Librarian
       Chartered Institute of Bankers
       10 Lombard Street
       London EC3V 9AS   Tel: 01-623 3531

British & Irish Association of Law
Librarians (BIALL)
Contact: Ms H.C. Boucher
       Librarian
       Pinsent & Co
       Post & Mail House
       26 Colmore Circus
       Birmingham B4 6BH   Tel: 021-200 1050

City Information Group
Contact: Nigel Oxbrow
       TFPL Ltd
       22 St Peter's Lane
       London EC1M 6DS   Tel: 01-251 5522

City Law Librarians' Group
Contact: Elisabeth Tooms
       Allen & Overy
       9 Cheapside
       London EC2V 6AD   Tel: 01-248 9898

Construction Industry Information Group (CIIG)
Contact: Marshall Crawford
       The Building Centre
       26 Store Street
       London WC1E 7BT   Written enquiries only.

Information for Energy Group
Contact: Mrs Jean Etherton
       Institute of Petroleum
       61 New Cavendish Street
       London W1M 8AR   Tel: 01-636 1004

Insurance Librarians and Information Officers' Group
Contact: Anna Leith
The Information Section
Association of British Insurers
Aldermary House
Queen Street
London EC4N 1TU   Tel: 01-248 4477

Marine Librarians Association
Contact: Alan Witherby
c/o Witherby & Co Ltd
32–36 Aylesbury Street
London EC1R 0ET   Tel: 01-253 5413

Property Information Group
Contact: Paul Lunn
The Research & Information Department
Estates Gazette
151 Wardour Street
London W1V 4BN   Tel: 01-437 0141

Sport and Recreation Information Group
Contact: Michele Shoebridge
Sports Documentation Centre
Main Library
University of Birmingham
Birmingham B15 2TT   Tel: 021-472 1301 (ext. 2312)

Appendix 2 • Organisations offering short courses in library and information work and related subjects

Aslib Professional Development
Information House
26–27 Boswell Street
London WC1N 3JZ
Tel: 01-430 2671

A wide range of courses on most aspects of information work.

Central Information Services
University of London
Senate House
Malet Street
London WC1
Tel: 01-636 8000

Individual and group tuition in the use of online services.

Centre for Information Science
The City University
Northampton Square
London EC1V 0HB
Tel: 01-253 4399

Courses on information handling in a variety of subject areas.

Industrial Society
Peter Runge House
3 Carlton House Terrace
London SW1Y 5DG
Tel: 01-839 4300

Training in various aspects of management and related skills.

Learned Information (Europe) Ltd
Woodside
Hinksey Hill
Oxford OX1 5AU
Tel: 0865 730275

Sponsors a major annual UK online conference.

Library Association
7 Ridgmount Street
London WC1E 7AE
Tel: 01-636 7543

Runs a number of seminars and short courses on library management and skills as well as on developments in the profession.

TFPL Ltd
22 St Peter's Lane
London EC1M 6DS
Tel: 01-251 5522

Wide range of courses, including in-company tailor-made ones, on all aspects of library and information work at all levels. Operates recruitment and publishing divisions.

A number of schools of library and information studies now offer short updating courses and seminars on current developments. For details of specific courses consult the publications mentioned throughout the text.

Appendix 3 • *Specialist publishers and book and periodical suppliers*

ABC International
World Timetable Centre
Church Street
Dunstable
Bedfordshire LU5 4HB
Tel: (0582) 600111

International travel and hotel guides.

Alan Armstrong Ltd
2 Arkwright Road
Reading RG2 0SQ
Tel: 0734 751855
and
6 Castle Street
Edinburgh EH2 3AT
Tel: 031-226 4201
Also in Washington DC

International bookseller to libraries and industry. UK enquiries to Reading office; export enquiries to Edinburgh.

Aslib, The Association for
Information Management
Information House
26–27 Boswell Street
London WC1N 3JZ
Tel: 01-430 2671

Publisher of books, journals and reports covering all aspects of establishing and maintaining efficient libraries and information services, including the use of external information sources such as online databases.

Barbican Business Book Centre
9 Moorfields .
London EC2Y 9AE
Tel: 01-628 7479

Blackwell's Bookshop
Broad Street
Oxford OX1 3BQ
Tel: (086ᶜ) 792792

Carries a large comprehensive stock in all subject fields, and gives a good postal service.

Business Surveys
PO Box 21
Dorking
Surrey RH4 2YU
Tel: (0306) 712867

Publishers of *Research Index* and *Reports Index*.

Collets Library Supply Service
Denington Estate
Wellingborough
Northants NN8 2QT
Tel: (0933) 224351

Provides worldwide service for supply of books, periodicals and audiovisual materials to all types of libraries, schools, booksellers and other agencies.

William Dawson Holdings plc
Cannon House
Park Farm Road
Folkstone
Kent CT19 5EE
Tel: (0303) 850101

Periodical subscriptions and automated serials control system to facilitate interlending.

Dillon's University Bookshop
1 Malet Street
London WC1
Tel: 01-637 1577

Offers a wide range of stock in all subject areas. Also has a mail order department.

Economist Bookshop
Clare Market
Portugal Street
London WC2
Tel: 01-405 5531

Although specialising in economic titles there is a good stock of general reference items.

Foyles
119 Charing Cross Road
London WC2
Tel: 01-437 5660

Large, wide-ranging stock on all subjects. Second-hand publications also available.

Government Bookshop (HMSO)
49 High Holborn
London WC1
Tel: 01-211 5656

Headland Press
1 Henry Smith's Terrace
Headland
Cleveland TS24 0PD
Tel: (0429) 231902

Specialist publishers to the library and information professions. Books and journals, annual conference. Excellent support service.

Industrial Society
Peter Runge House
3 Carlton House Terrace
London SW1 5DG
Tel: 01-839 4300

The Society's own publications, many in pamphlet form, on matters relating to staff and the work environment, are available direct from their publications department.

Institute of Personnel Management
IPM House
Camp Road
London SW19 4UW
Tel: 01-946 9100

The IPM produces a wide range of publications on all aspects of personnel management, which can be purchased direct from the Institute.

H.K. Lewis
136 Gower Street
London WC1E 6BS
Tel: 01-387 4282

Specialises in medical and scientific books.

Library Association Publishing Ltd
7 Ridgmount Street
London WC1E 7AE
Tel: 01-636 7543

Marketing Surveys Index
32 Mill Green Road
Mitcham
Surrey CR4 4HY
Tel: 01-640 6621

Market and business research directory.

Parks
244 High Holborn
London WC1V 7DZ
Tel: 01-831 9501/2

Concentrates on accounting, banking, business and law books.

Professional Publishing Ltd
7 Swallow Place
London W1R 8AB
Tel: 01-409 3322

Handles all the publications of the British Institute of Management, as well as other business and legal publications. No retail outlet. Orders are dealt with only by post.

Swets United Kingdom Ltd
32 Blacklands Way
Abingdon Business Park
Abingdon
Oxford OX14 1SX
Tel: (0235) 30809

Offers a comprehensive library supply service. Handles books and periodicals on an international basis. The service offers speedy response through its automated systems. (Headquarters in Amsterdam.)

J. Whitaker & Sons Ltd
12 Dyott Street
London WC1A 1DF
Tel: 01-836 8911

Publishers of *British Books in Print*, the *Bookseller* and a range of major bibliographies in printed form, microfiche and CD-ROM.

Graham Wyche & Associates
71 Oakwood Crescent
Winchmore Hill
London N21 1PA
Tel: 01-360 1318

Specialises in accountancy, taxation, legal and government publications. The emphasis is on quick, personal service.

To trace further book suppliers consult the *Directory of specialist bookdealers in the UK handling mainly new books* as shown in the Core List at the end of Chapter 3.

Appendix 4 • Library equipment suppliers

Balmforth Engineering Ltd
Library Systems Division
Finway
Dallow Road
Luton
Bedfordshire LU1 1TE
Tel: (0582) 31171

Don Gresswell Ltd
Bridge House
Grange Park
London N21 1RB
Tel: 01-360 6622

Libraco Ltd
Warspite Road
London SE18 5NX
Tel: 01-855 6102

Library Design and Engineering Ltd
44 Gloucester Avenue
London NW1 8JD
Tel: 01-722 0111

Templestock Ltd
Systems House
1 Ravenscourt Park
London W6 0TZ
Tel: 01-741 0625/7
(also offers complete planning service)

Terrapin Reska Ltd
Bond Avenue
Bletchley
Milton Keynes MK1 1JJ
Tel: (0908) 270900

Details of other suppliers of library equipment and furniture can be traced by looking at *Kompass* (see the Core List at the end of Chapter 3); or by consulting the collections of library equipment catalogues at Aslib and at the Library Equipment Centre located at the College of Librarianship Wales.

Index

Abstracts, 10, 61, 62
Accession numbers, 69
   register (illus.), 68
Administrative procedures, 10 – 11, 34 – 35,
   50 – 55, 64 – 72
   see also Manual of procedures
Appraisal interviews, 96
Approval copies, 57, 58, 85, 89
Author index, 73

Bibliographical sources, 59 – 61
   see also Core list; Publishers' catalogues
Bliss Bibliographic Classification
   scheme, 80
Book card (illus.), 83
Booksuppliers, see suppliers
BP Chemicals classification scheme, 79
Budget planning, 10, 17 – 18, 20, 47,
   51 – 52, 69
Bulletins 21, 48, 61 – 63, 97
   see also scanning
Business information 58 – 59, 98 – 101
   Sources of specific types of information
   are shown in App. 1 and the Core
   List on pp. 21 – 29
   see also Online services

Cataloguing, 10, 15, 48, 52, 72, 73 – 77
   slip, 76 (illus.), 76 – 77
CD-ROM, 43 – 44
Checklists, see individual subject headings
   and contents page
Circulation of stock, see Stock
Classification, 9, 15, 52, 70, 77 – 81
   checklist, 80 – 81
   evaluation, 80 – 81
   schemes, 77 – 80
Collection management, 44 – 47
Colour, use of, 54 – 55, 62, 85
Communication, 2, 19, 62, 92, 97
   see also Presentations
Company information, see Business
   information
Computers, 12, 18, 35, 36 ,37, 38 – 49, 69,
   70, 74, 79, 80, 88, 97, 98, 100 – 101
Consultants, use of, 19, 32
Contacts, see External resources; Groups
Contents pages, circulation of, 61
Core list, 16 – 17, 21 – 29, 56 – 57
Correspondence, 11, 52
Costs, see Budget planning
Courses, 19, 93 – 94, 102, App. 2.

Daily routines, 51
Data protection, 47, App. 1
Departmental collections, 7, 12
Dewey Decimal Classification, 79
Dictionary catalogue, 74, 75, 79
Display, 63

Economic information, see Business
   information
Electronic mail, 46 – 47
Enquiry work, 41 – 42, 45 – 46, 92 – 93
Environmental factors, 11 – 12
   see also Physical planning
Equipment, 18, 30 – 37, 38 – 40, 101
   checklists, 31 – 32, 36 – 37
   see also Physical planning; Suppliers
Essential material, 7
   basic list, 21 – 29
Essential tasks, see Immediate action
   checklist
Existing resources checklist, 9 – 12
External resources, 7, 12 – 14, 19, 53,
   59 – 60, 100 – 101

Formal groups, see Groups
Free material, 59 – 60
Furniture, 11
   see also Physical planning

Government publications, 59 – 60
   see also Core List; Business information
Groups, 13 – 14, 19, 93, 101 – 102
Guides to library service, 51, 98

Heating, 11
   see also Physical planning

Immediate action, 19 – 20
   checklist, 20
Indexing services, 10, 60 – 61, 100, 101
Informal groups, see Groups
Information
   bulletins, 21, 61 – 63, 78, 97
   files, see Subject files
   needs analysis, 2, 3, 4 – 6, 21;
     checklist, 6
   services, 53, 100, 101
   technology, 19, 38 – 49
   see also External resources; Online
     services; Word processors
In-house publications, 7, 17, 100
Initial service, 15 – 29

Initial tasks, *see* Immediate action checklist
Interlibrary loan, 10, 85, 87 – 88, 98
Internal resources, 8 – 12
Introductory talks, *see* Presentations
Invoices, 10, 52, 65 – 66, 69

Job satisfaction, 91, 94, App. 1
Job sharing, 95, App. 1
Journals, 52, 56, 57, 60, 61, 69, 80 – 87, 88
   core list, 17, 27 – 29
   storage, 31, 34, 36

Keywords, use of, 15, 53, 77

Labels, *see* Notices and labels
Layout of library, 13, 54 – 55
   see also Physical planning
Library of Congress classification
   scheme, 80
Library service
   criteria, 15, 51
   guides to, 51, 98
Lighting, 11
   see also Physical planning
Loan systems, 10, 52, 82 – 88
   cards, 54, 83 (illus.)
   slip, 84 (illus.), 85 (illus.), 86 (illus.)
Location, 8
   see also Physical planning
London Classification of Business Studies, 78
Looseleaf services, 52, 58, 69, 72
   Specific titles shown in Core List, 21 – 29

Manual of procedures, 11, 48, 50 – 53, 90, 94
   checklist, 51 – 53
Marketing information, *see* Business
   information
Microfiche and microfilm, 9, 36 – 37, 58, 74

Newsletters, 21, 61 – 62, 97
Newspapers, 21, 48, 52, 58, 60
   see also Scanning
Notice boards, 63
Notices and labels, 54 – 55

Office collections, *see* Departmental
   collections
One person libraries, 13, 15, 94
   definition, 61
Online services, 9, 16, 18, 30, 41 – 43, 61,
   95, 100 – 101, App. 1, App. 2
   checklist, 42

Ordering procedures and stationery, 48,
   54 – 55, 64 – 69, 71 – 72
   card, 66 (illus.)
   form, 65 (illus.)
   slip, 67 (illus.)
Organisation profile, 1, 2
   checklist, 2 – 3

Periodicals
   Core List, 27 – 29
   see also Journals
Personal contact, *see* User contact
Physical planning, 13, 30 – 37, App. 4
   checklists, 9 – 12. 31 – 32, 36 – 37
Presentations, 16, 51, 54, 97, 98
Press cuttings services (internal), 62, 98
   see also Information services
Procedures, *see* Administrative procedures
Processing, *see* Stock
Progress reports, 16, 19, 53
Publicity, 16, 19, 48, 54, 97
   see also Presentations; User contact
Publishers' catalogues, 17, 58 – 59

Recent additions list, 61
Records, *see* Administrative procedures;
   Stationery
Reference material, 17 – 19
   Core List, 21 – 29
   guides to, 17, 60
   'quick', 78
Registrations of material, *see* Stock,
   processing

Scanning, 61 – 63, 94
Seating, 11
   see also Physical planning
Selective Dissemination of Information, 98
Shelving, *see* Physical planning
Spreadsheets, 20, 45 – 46
Staff, 12, 50 – 51, 102
   costs, 17 – 18
   qualities, 1, 91 – 96
   time, charging for, 18, 47
Standards
   accounting, 77, 78
   technical, 60, App. 1
Stationery, 34 – 35, 48, 54 – 55, 64 – 71,
   82 – 89, App. 4
   see also specific procedures
Statistical information, *see* Business
   information

Stock, 18, 56 – 72, 82 – 90
  circulation, 48, 52 – 53, 56 – 57, 61, 69, 88 – 89
  Core List, 21 – 29
  effective use, 61 – 63
  format, 9, 57 – 58
    checklist, 36 – 37
  initial, 16 – 17, 21 – 29
  processing, 52, 70 – 71, 82 – 83
  review form, 89
  selection and acquisition, 10, 18 – 19, 56 – 61, 64 – 69
  storage checklist, 36 – 37
  see also headings for specific types of material, e.g. loan, reference, journals; and specific procedures
Storage, *see* Physical planning
Study carrell, 35 (illus.)
Subject files, 34 (illus.), 7, 33, 52, 54, 61, 62
Subject headings, 75
Subject index, 73

Suppliers, 31 – 32, 34, 53, 64, 71 – 72, 74, App. 3, App. 4
  checklist of criteria, 72

Timetable for setting up, 19 – 20
Title index, 73
Tracings, 75
Training, *see* Courses

Universal Decimal Classification, 79 – 80
User contact, 1, 16, 47, 54 – 55, 61 – 63, 91 – 92, 97 – 99

Ventilation, 11, 31
Visible index, 69, 74, 77, 86 – 87, 86 (illus.)
Visits to other libraries, 14

Word processor, use of, 11, 35, 36 – 37, 48, 62, 69, 74, 79, 88, 100
Working collection, *see* Departmental collections

3 5282 00137 7020